C000241211

London Midland Region Track Diagr

This is the fourth atlas of a series to cover all British Rail lines and includes twenty-six private railways and museums. In general, it is up-to-date to October 1990.

Mileages often vary slightly between different official records, but those given have been taken from Civil Engineers' drawings, which are measured in yards. Station mileages are taken from the mid-point of the platforms, or in the case of a terminus, the buffer stops.

These diagrams have been compiled substantially from information supplied from British Rail Sources, supplemented by other data and amended from extensive field checks. In some cases distinctions between BR ownership and other parties are not shown and no inferences concerning ownership should be drawn.

The assistance of numerous BR officials, Associated British Ports, Dr Iain Frew, John Stratton and the undernoted railway companies is gratefully acknowledged.

Bala Lake Railway	Great Central Railway	Ravensglass & Eskdale Railway
Birmingham Railway Museum	Gwili Railway	Severn Valley Railway
Brecon Mountain Railway	Lakeside & Haverthwaite Rly	Talyllyn Railway
East Lancashire Light Railway	Leighton Buzzard Railway	Welshpool & Llanfair Railway
Ffestiniog Railway	Llanberis Lake Railway	Yorkshire Dales Railway
Foxfield Light Railway	Llangollen Railway	
Gloucestershire Warwickshire Rly	Northamptonshire Ironstone Rly	

Cartographer: John Yonge   Consultant editor and liaison with BR: Gerald Jacobs

KEY

———	Running line	
———	Siding	
—I—	Regional boundary	
—!—	Signal box area limits	
BJ | SY SB | PSB		
→- - -←	Tunnel	
—+—	Level crossing	
←—→	Track signalled in both directions (a double arrow indicates normal direction of travel)	
—Ջ—	Private siding boundary, often marked by a gate	
wwww	Wall	
●—●—●	Gantry Rails	

93 ǀ	Whole mileposts, shown on the appropriate side of the line
▪3	Platform with number
▭	Platform out of use
⊠(EN)	Signal box with code
▪	Gate box
▫	Ground frame
o	Lineside telephone (not shown at level crossings and stations)
⊙	Water Tower
^	Summit
86.34	Distance in miles and chains (80 chains to 1 mile; 22 yards – about 20 metres – equal 1 chain)
LEC	ELR (Engineers Line Reference)

PRICE : £6.95
ISBN : 0 900609 74 5

Published by the Quail Map Company, 2 Lincoln Road, Exeter EX4 2DZ Tel/Fax: 01392 430277 and printed by Vine & Gorfin Ltd., Exmouth, Devon. © Quail Map Company. October 1990. Reprinted September 1996 by Brightsea Press, Exeter.

Cover photograph: The 11.25 Birmingham New Street to Pwllheli service departs from Shrewsbury after reversal on 29th June 1990, formed by Class 150/1 'Sprinter' no. 150124. (© Brian Morrison)

ABBREVIATIONS

ABCL	Automatic Barrier Crossing Locally monitored		L & NW	London & North Western
ABP	Associated British Ports		LPG	Liquid petroleum gas
AC	Alternating current		LS	Loco shed
AHB	Automatic half-barriers		LU	London Underground Ltd.
AOCL	Automatic Open Crossing Locally monitored by train crew		MD & HC	Mersey Docks & Harbour Co.
			M & EE	Mechanical & Electrical Engineer
AOCR	Automatic Open Crossing Remotely monitored by signalman		MGR	Merry-go-round
			MOD	Ministry of Defence
			MSC	Manchester Ship Canal
AR	Anglia Region		MU	Maintenance Unit
ARR	Arrival		N	North
BC	British Coal (ex NCB – National Coal Board)		NIRU	Not in regular use
			OTM	On-track Traction Maintenance
BCH	Branch		OOU	Out of use
BR	British Rail		ps	Private siding
CCD	Coal Concentration Depot		PSB	Power signal box
CCTV	Closed circuit television		PTE	Passenger Transport Executive
CE	Civil Engineer		PW	Permanent Way
CL	Crossing Loop		RC	Remotely controlled
COM	Change of mileage		REC	Reception
CR	Cripple siding		RG	Miniature Red/Green Warning Lights
CW	Carriage washer			
C & W	Carriage & wagon		RR	Run-round
DC	Direct current		S	South
DEP	Departure		SB	Signal box
DF	Down Fast		SC	Signalling Centre
DG	Down Goods		SCC	Signalling Control Centre
DGL	Down Goods Loop		ScR	Scottish Region
DL	Down Loop		SD	Sand Drag
DM	Down Main		Sdg(s)	Siding(s)
DMU	Diesel Multiple Unit		SF	Shunting Frame
DN	Down		SN	Shunt neck
DPL	Down passenger loop		SR	Southern Region
DRS	Down refuge siding		TA	Tamper Siding
DS	Down Slow		TB	Turnback Siding
DT	Down Through		TMD	Traction Maintenance Depot
E	East		TMO	Trainmen Operated
EMU	Electric multiple-unit		T & RS	Traction & Rolling Stock
ER	Eastern Region		UF	Up Fast
FP	Fuelling point		UG	Up Goods
GC	Gantry Crane		UGL	Up Goods loop
GF	Ground Frame		UL	Up loop
GS	Goods Shed		UM	Up Main
H	Headshunt		UPL	Up Passenger loop
HH	Hopper House		URS	Up Refuge Siding
Jn	Junction		US	Up Slow
LC	Level Crossing		UT	Up Through
LMR	London Midland Region		W	West
			WB	Weighbridge
			yds	yards

In the same series:
1. ScotRail £2.50
2. Eastern & Anglia Regions £5.00
3. Western Region £5.00
5. Southern Region & London Underground *(in preparation)*
The Quail Map Company produces and imports railway maps of various countries and cities. A catalogue will be sent on request.

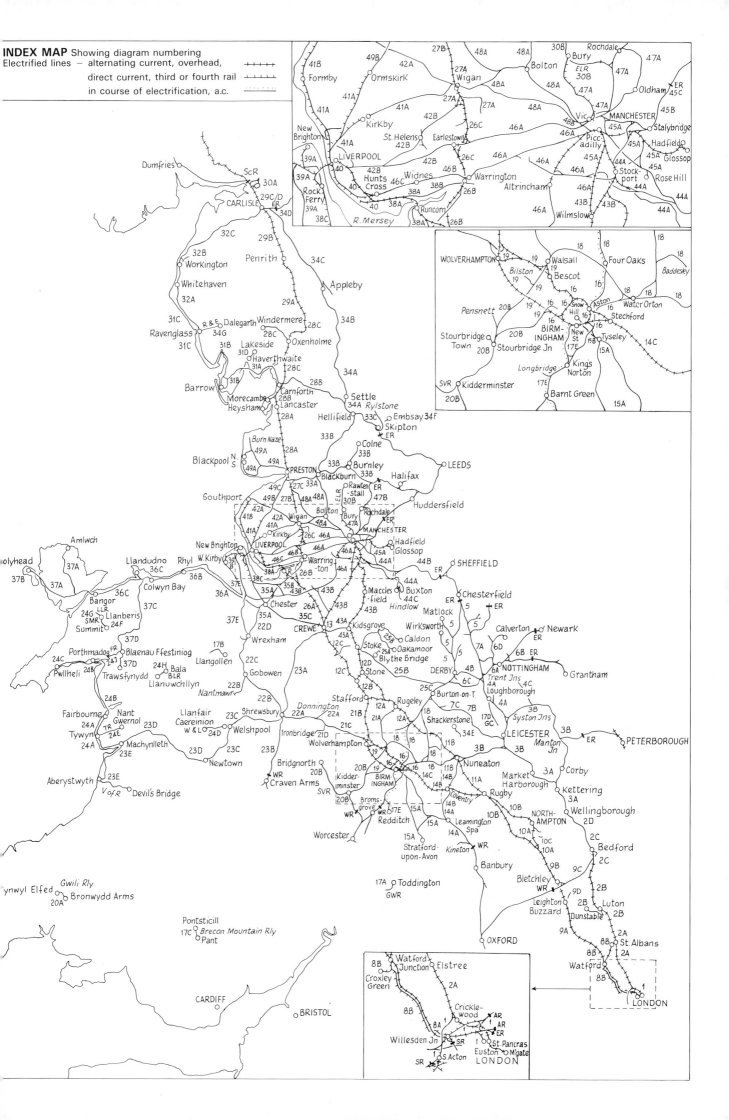

INDEX MAP Showing diagram numbering

Electrified lines — alternating current, overhead,

direct current, third or fourth rail

in course of electrification, a.c.

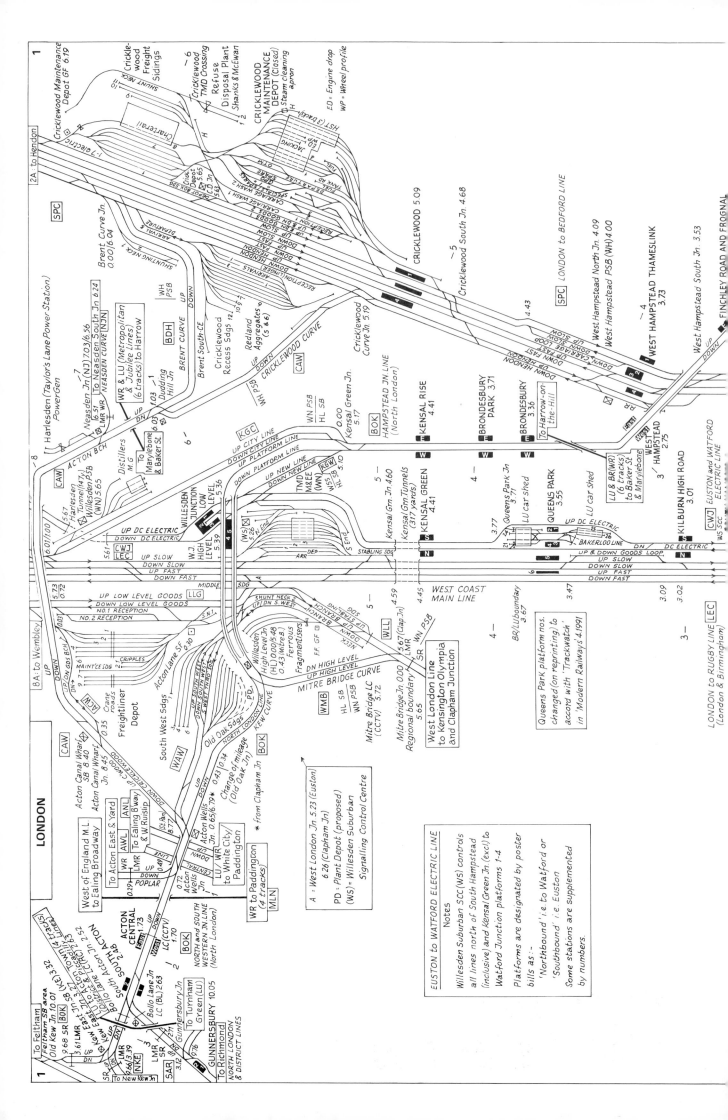

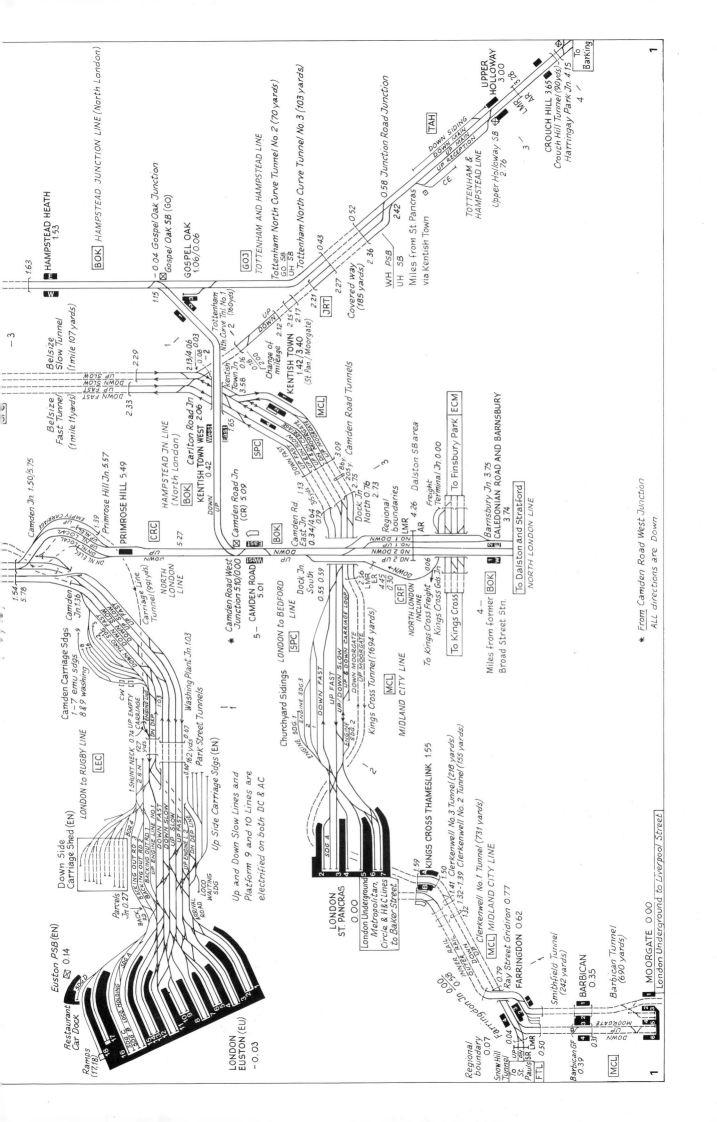

MIDLAND LINE : HENDON - BEDFORD - WELLINGBOROUGH ● DUNSTABLE BRANCH

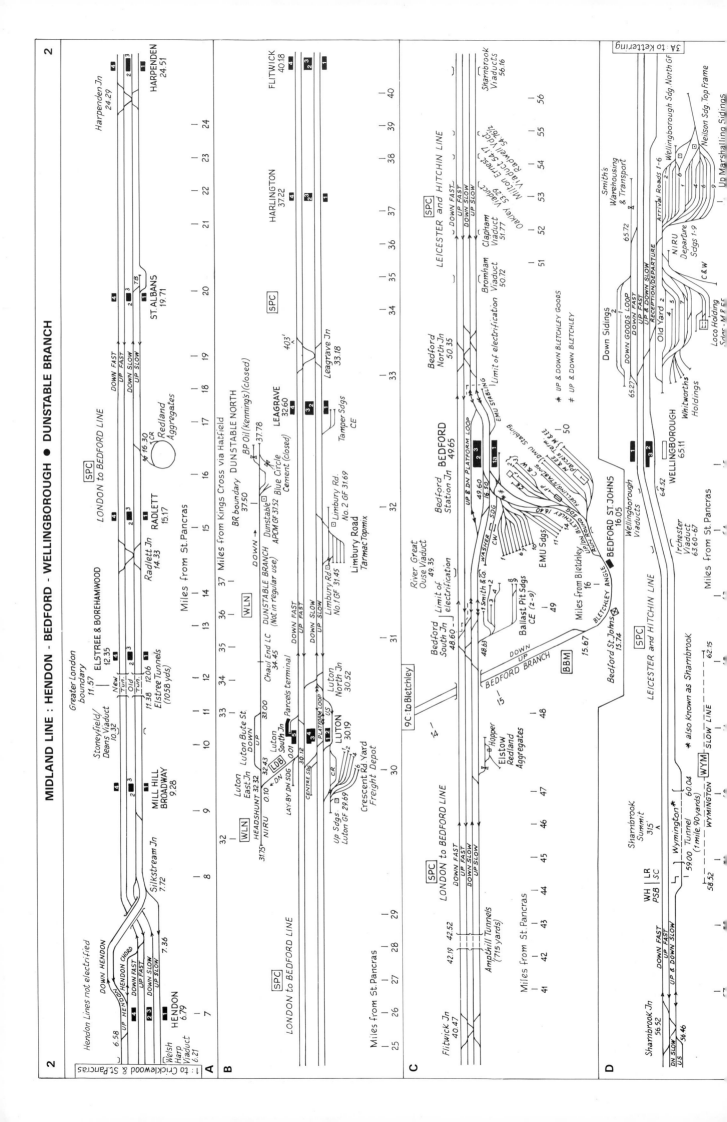

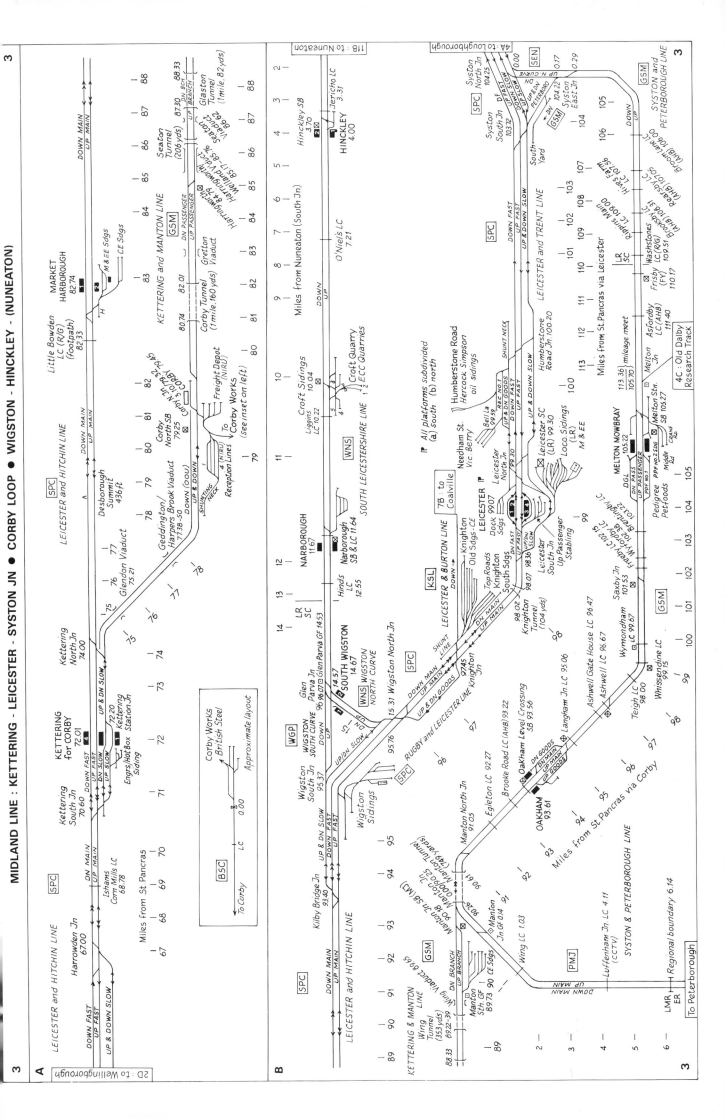

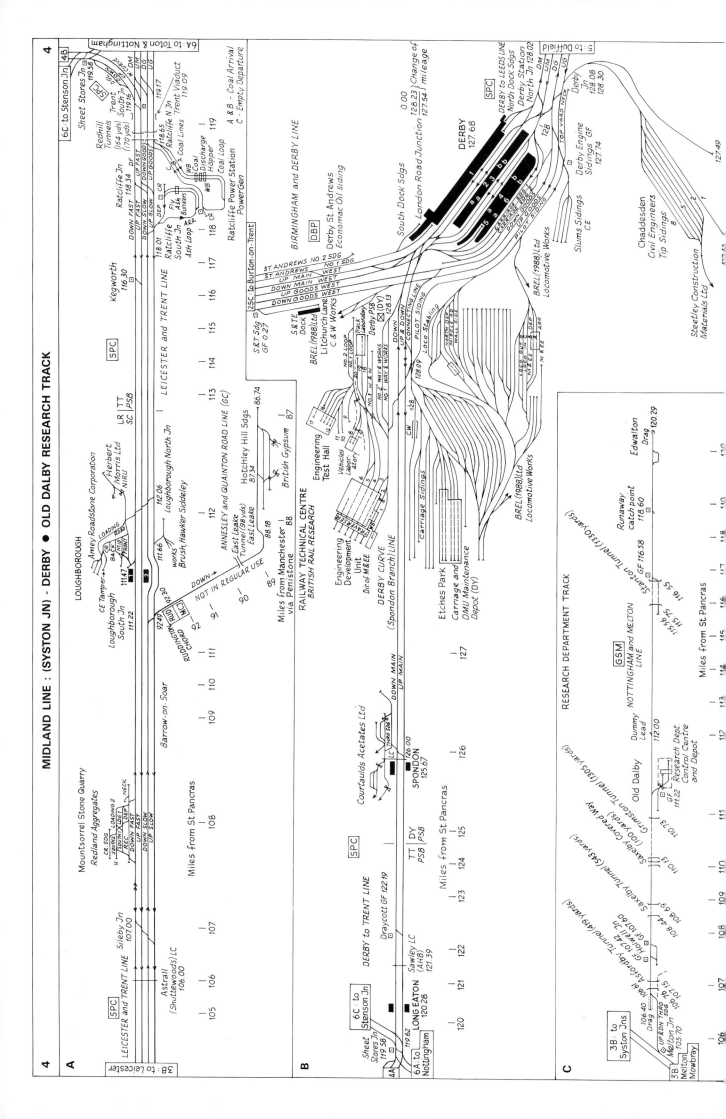

MIDLAND LINE : (SYSTON JN) - DERBY ● OLD DALBY RESEARCH TRACK

WIRKSWORTH QUARRY

Tarmac Ltd

WIRKSWORTH

THE GULLY

Wirksworth Station GF 141.21

Gorsey Bank LC (AOCL) 140.79

Idridgehay LC (AOCL) 138.08

WIRKSWORTH BRANCH (not in regular use)

DOWN →

Incline GF 141.45

Incline

River Amber Viaduct 138.26

Ambergate Jn 137d River Derwent Viaduct

AMBERGATE 138.18

Ambergate CE
Ambergate GF 138.35

Toadmoor Tnl (129yds)

Whatstandwell Tnl (149yds)

WHATSTANDWELL 140.13
High Peak Junction Lea Wood Tnl (315 yards) 141.42-56

Wingfield Tunnel (261 yards)

Whatstandwell 141.42-56

Peak Rail ps

GF 145.26

MATLOCK 145.00
GF 145.03
High Tor No.1 Tunnel (764 yards)
Willersley Tunnel (765 yards)
Willersley BATT (31 yards)
No.4 Tunnel (58 yards)
Holloway (126 yds)
Cromford Viaduct 143.03-143.06
Cromford 143.10
143.13-.48
AJM

Lovers Walk
Boathouse Bridge 144.60

AMBERGATE and ROWSLEY LINE

RD = River Derwent Viaduct 140.51

DERBY to LEEDS LINE

Little Eaton Jn

Derby PSB area

Duffield Jn 132.79
Duffield Tunnel (52 yds)
DUFFIELD 133.08
Little Eaton Station LC (TMO)

Milford Tunnel (855 yds)
BELPER 135.55
Belper GF 134.61
Belper CE

Broadholme 136.48

Denby North LC (TMO) 135.46
Denby Street Lane LC (TMO) 135.73

Coxbench LC (TMO) 133.03
Holbrook LC (TMO) 133.23

Kilburn LC (TMO) 134.75

RIPLEY BRANCH DOWN →

DENBY DISPOSAL POINT
British Coal
'Hargreaves Industrial Service'

Butterley Works

Museum
Road Transport Museum
Modern Traction Depot (proposed)
Loco repair dept.
Carriage shed
Historic carriage & wagon repairs

MIDLAND RAILWAY TRUST LTD.

BUTTERLEY

HAMMERSMITH
RR S&T Depot
causeway

SWANWICK JN
Swanwick Spur (wagon storage)

Golden Valley Halt (proposed)
Riddings (opening 4/1991)

Pye Bridge Jn 133.67
Coates Park 134.40
Sleights East
Pinxton SB & LC 134.76
Langton Colliery Branch Jn
Pinxton SB & LC 135.46
Langton Colliery Jn 135.52

ALFRETON & MANSFIELD PARKWAY
Blackwell Sth. Jn 136.07
Alfreton Tunnel (840 yards) 135.11
Swanwick Jn 135.50

Tibshelf & Blackwell Branch Jn

Alfreton Explosives & Chemical Co.
Tibshelf GF 136.27
Tibshelf GF 136.36

'400' Morton 139.06
Doe Hill
Shell GF 138.32
Appleyard Fuels

TIBSHELF and TEVERSALL LINE
Tibshelf LC (open) 137.70

AVENUE COKING PLANT
National Smokeless Fuels Ltd
7 = Loaded wagon sdgs. 1-7
8/9 = Empty wagon arrival
10 = Run-round

Coking Plant GF
Hopper Controller & Retarder
BR loco limit
144.68 LMR ER

COAL DEP
COAL ARR

Hasland 144.15
Avenue Sdgs GF 143.30 OOU
Hasland Xover OOU

Horns Bridge
Regional boundary

To Chesterfield

DERBY to LEEDS LINE (North Midland)

SPC

Clay Cross North Jn
Clay Cross Tunnel (1 mile, 24 yards)
Clay Cross South Jn 142.10
146.21

Coney Green Jn 141.24

Stretton GF 145.34

DY PSB / TT PSB

EREWASH VALLEY LINE
TCC

SILVERHILL COLLIERY
British Coal
SCB
loading bunker
141.61
Token Cabin
Silverhill 141.74
Sutton Colliery 140.34
former Sutton Colliery
Sutton Colliery Jn GF
SKEGBY BRANCH

Sherwood Colliery
British Coal - Sherwood Colliery
Sherwood Vadct. Pad
Mansfield Vadct. Pad
WB Sdgs North GF
WB Sdgs. Sth GF
141.49 141.73
143.40 LMR ER
PBS

To Shirebrook

Sutton Jn Stn
Sutton Forest LC
Sutton-in-Ashfield
Sutton Jn LC (TMO) 138.23 (AHB)
Sutton Jn. SB
Hermitage Mill LC 138.33 (AHB)
0.42
0.66
138.50 Change of mileage 138
Kirkby Summit 137.11
138.79

Kirkby LC (TMO) 0.42

Bentinck Colliery
British Coal
Bunker

Codnor Park Jn
Ironville RR
Codnor Park Jn 132.76

Riddings
RR
Codnor Park
Codnor Park GF 131.53
Codnor Park Sdgs GF 132.37

Miles from St Pancras

LANGLEY MILL 129.68

Langley Mill GF 129.77
Stoneyford GF 131.53

ERENWASH VALLEY LINE
TCC

DERBY to LEEDS LINE
SPC

UP DEP SDG
St. Marys South Jn
Nottingham Road Viaduct 128.40
128.53 DN REC
129.06 St. Marys North Jn
129.17
129.33
Derby Corporation
Thomas Hill Foundries

DOWN MAIN
UP MAIN
DOWN GOODS
UP GOODS

Lower Portland Farm LC 136.27
Upper Portland LC (AHB) 136.71

PINXTON BRANCH
PBS

Route descriptions between # signs :-

Y = NOTTINGHAM and MANSFIELD LINE
Z = MANSFIELD and WORKSOP BRANCH

48: to Derby

7A: to Toton

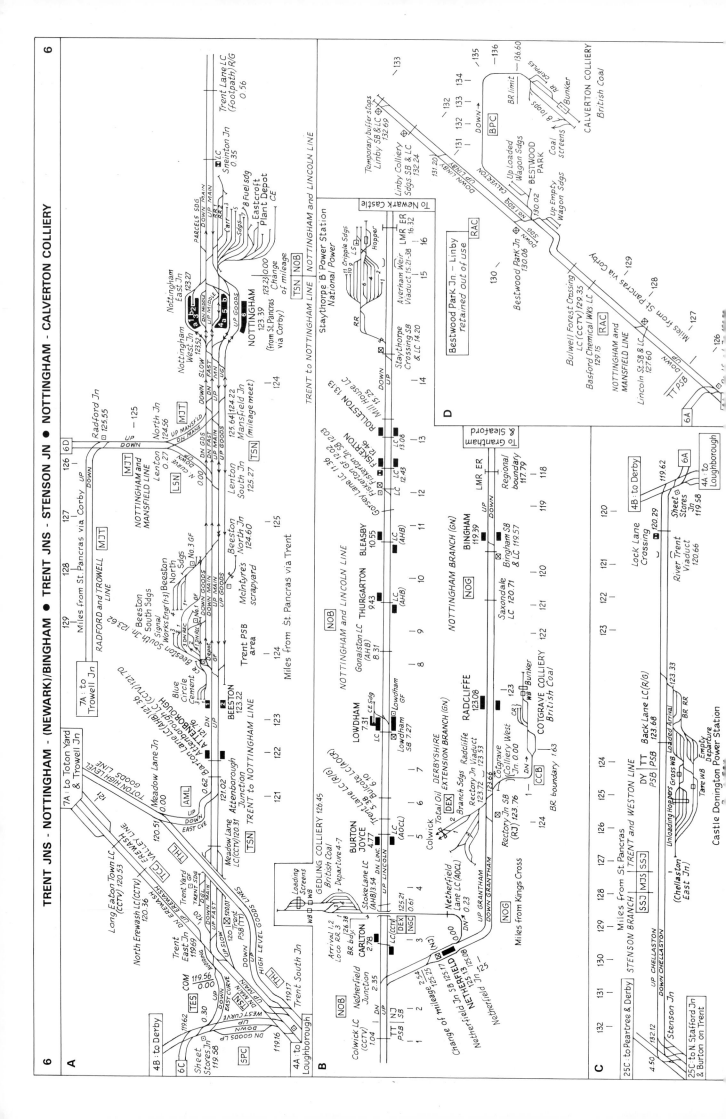

TRENT JNS - NOTTINGHAM - (NEWARK)/BINGHAM ● TRENT JNS - STENSON JN ● NOTTINGHAM - CALVERTON COLLIERY

MIDLAND LINE : TOTON - (LANGLEY MILL) ● LEICESTER - BURTON LINE : (KNIGHTON JN) - BIRMINGHAM CURVE JN

A

FA = Fuel Avoiding Line   WL = Wheel lathe
F1, F2 = Nos 1 and 2 Fuel Roads   WP = Washing plants
T = Tank Road

Sandiacre Ballast Sidings
STAPLEFORD and SANDIACRE

5: to Langley Mill

TCC EREWASH VALLEY LINE

Long Eaton
United Transport Oils

Meadow Sdgs

Down Marshalling North Yard Sidings (two systems of numbering) 20/16
33/3

Minor Materials Depot T.W. Ward scrapyard
Rugby Cement

TMD (TO) M & EE
Loco Stabling Sdgs

RECEPTION

Toton Jn
121.26
121.36

Traction Maintenance School

Old Bank Sidings - West Storage

Stapleford & Sandiacre
SF 122.35
122.47

Arrival Lines

Hump Avoiding Engine Line

Braunstone Gate (scrapyards)

Toton Centre GF
121.64

9 Fan no. 2

TOTON YARD

ERewash Valley Line
Toton Town (CCTV) Jn

DOWN HIGH LEVEL GOODS LINE
UP GOODS
SHUNT NECK WEST

THL

6A: to Trent Jns

Stanton & Staveley Works Sdg

Ilkeston GF 126.38

Stanton Gate 123.65
Stanton Gate South 123.31
Down Sdgs
WHM

Stanton Gate North Jn

Trowell Jn 125.09 / 130.56 (via Nottingham)
-130
MJT

6A: to Radford Jn & Nottingham
RADFORD and TROWELL LINE

TCC

Rapid loading bunker 127.35
127.31

Bennerley Opencast British Coal 128

129

ERewash Valley Line

124.19

Up Sidings
RECEPTION LINES
GF 123.12

Miles from St. Pancras
122 123 124 125 126 127

B

Aylestone Viaduct 98.35

Saffron Lane GF 98.02
Saffron Lane Power Station PowerGen

CHORD LINE

UP & DOWN BURTON

Vic Berry Ltd

F Berry Ltd · A.E.Piggott & Co

3B: to Knighton Jn

Kirby Muxloe LC 102.35
KSL

LEICESTER and BURTON LINE

Desford LC (AHB) 104.65

Bagworth Jn
REFUGE SDG 0.00
109.74

Cliffe Hill No 2 GF 110.42 / No 1 GF 110.63
Tarmac Ltd

Weighbridge 0.62
Stud Farm Quarry Tarmac Roadstone
CRIPPLES 1.24
Loading point 1.10

LR | BH
SC | SB
565 ft

Coalfields Farm - British Coal
Bunker
Shed CR
Coalfields Farm GF 0.62 / 0.00

Bardon Hill (BH) 111.23
Bardon Hill GF 111.40
Bardon Hill Quarries Prismo Universal Ltd (bitumen)

BH | ML
SB | SB

Coalville Jn 112.13

Coalville Station LC (CCTV-ML) 112.62
UP GDS
DN. GDS

Miles from St. Pancras
98 99 100 101 102 103 104 105 106 107 108 109 110 111 112

C

DRAKELOW POWER STATIONS PowerGen
'A' & 'B' Stations
'C' Station
Hoppers
Ash Coal Sdgs
Hopper
RECEPTIONS
A & B ARRIVAL

River Trent
To Birmingham
Drakelow West Curve Jn 125.62
Drakelow East Curve Jn 125.17
Drakelow Flood Viaduct 125.78
25C To Burton on Trent
To Branston 126.40

Coalville Station LC (CCTV-ML) 112.62
Marcroft Engineering
Mantle Lane (ML) 113.05
Coalville Town
GF 113.21 / 113.30
C & W
DOCK

Swannington LC (AHB) 114.01

Lounge Disposal Point British Coal
LOADING
Bunker CRIPPLE SDG
ML | MW
SB | SB

Lounge Jn 116.60 / 116.67

Moira West Jn (MW) 120.67

Rawdon Colliery - British Coal
Rawdon GF
Bunker
Screens 121
Rawdon Connectional Sidings

MW | DY
SB | PSB 121.62
121.11

Gresley Tunnel (623 yards) 122.10

KSL (Swadlincote Jn)

LEICESTER & BURTON LINE
DOWN GOODS
UP GOODS

Miles from St. Pancras
113 114 115 116 117 118 119 120 121 122 123 124 125 126

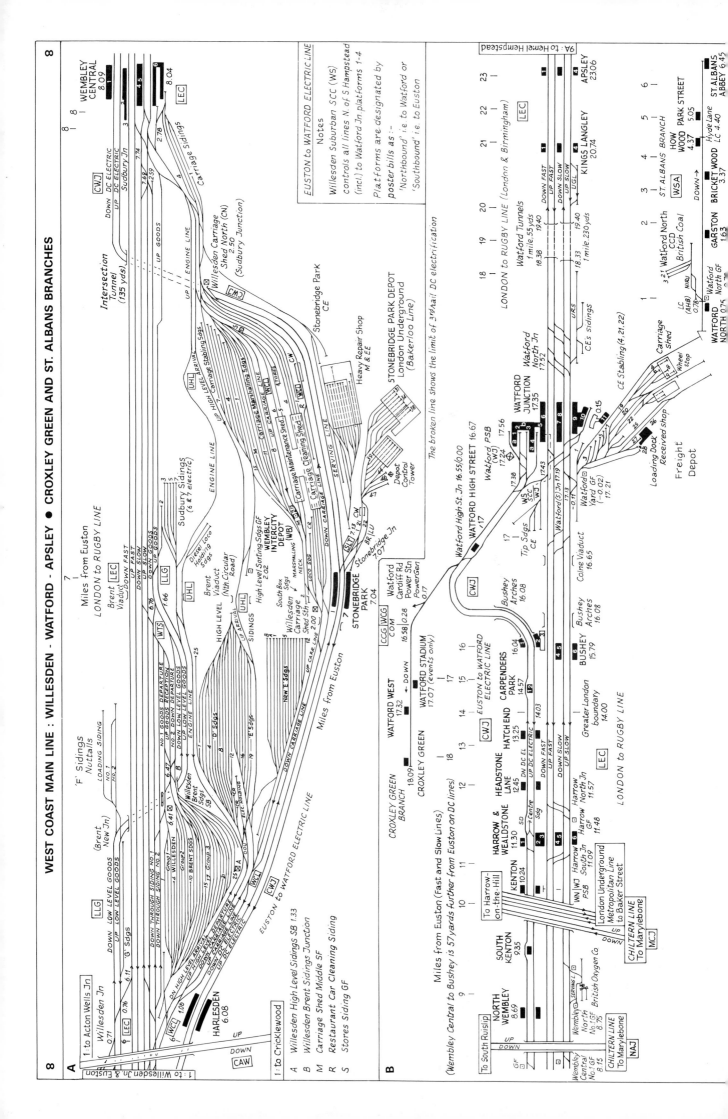

WEST COAST MAIN LINE : WILLESDEN - WATFORD - APSLEY ● CROXLEY GREEN AND ST. ALBANS BRANCHES

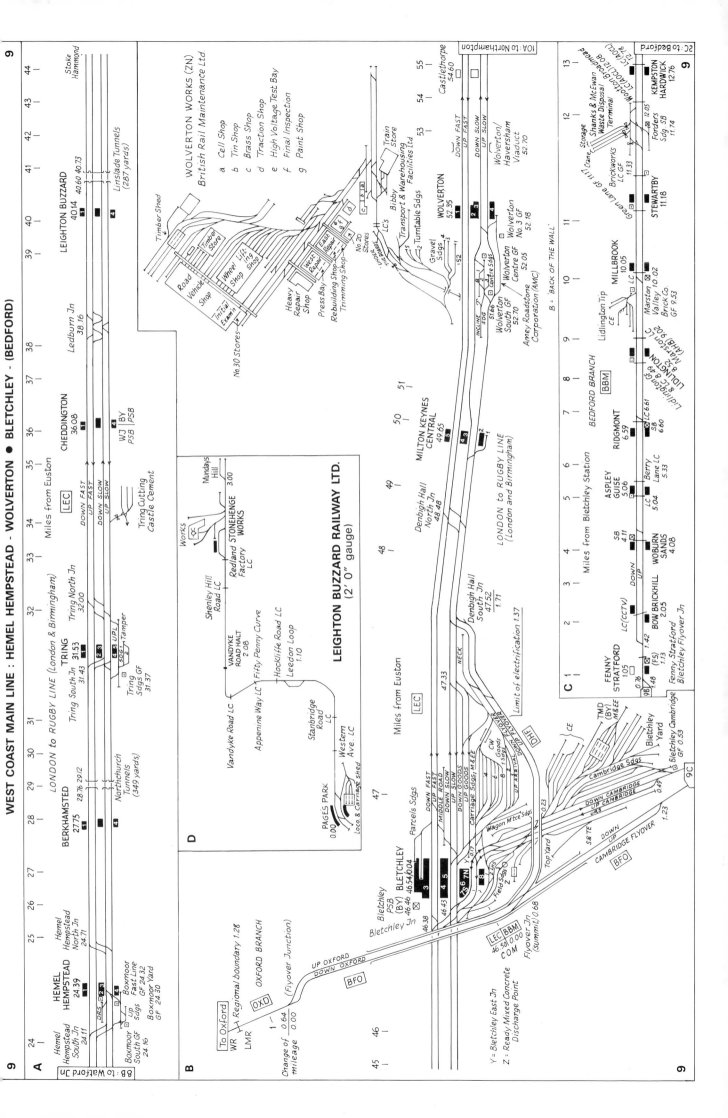

WEST COAST MAIN LINE : HEMEL HEMPSTEAD - WOLVERTON ● BLETCHLEY - (BEDFORD)

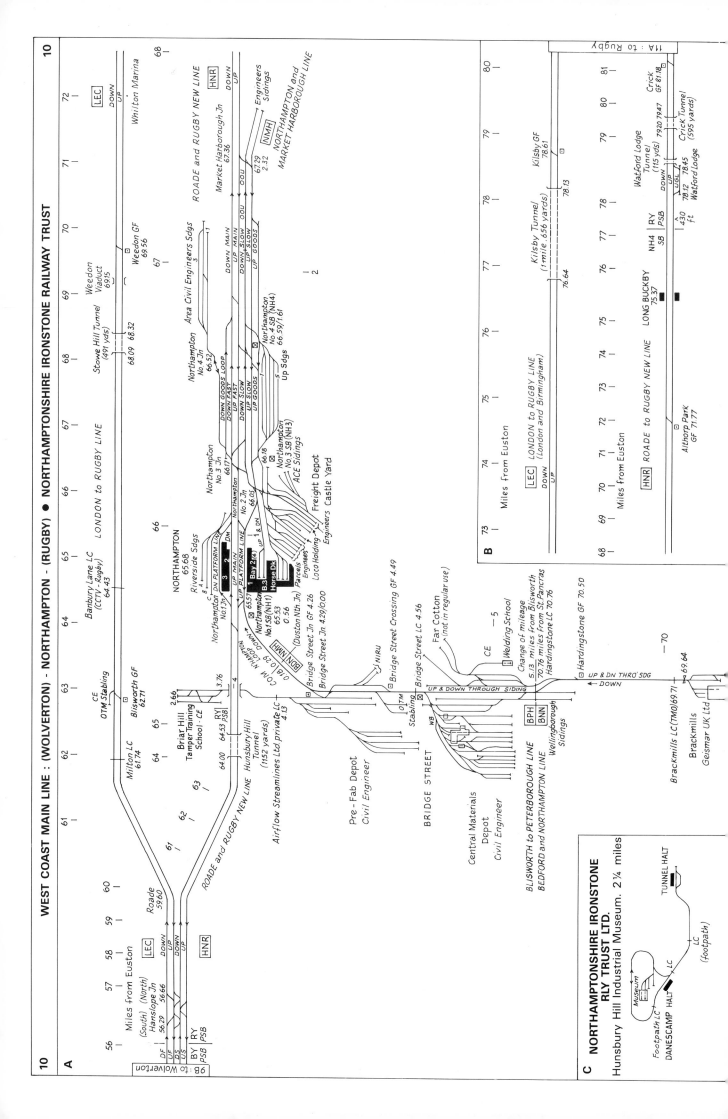

WEST COAST MAIN LINE : RUGBY - NUNEATON - TAMWORTH

A

RUGBY AND BIRMINGHAM LINE (London and Birmingham)

TRENT VALLEY LINE

Miles from Euston

80 81 82 83 84 85 86 87 88 89 90 91 92 93

Shilton 91.60

Nettle Hill Viaduct 89.51

Brinklow 87.72

RY | NN
PSB | PSB

LEC

DOWN FAST
UP SLOW
UP & DOWN SLOW
DOWN FAST
UP & DOWN FAST

Avon Viaduct 84.05

14B : to Coventry | RUGBY and BIRMINGHAM LINE (London and Birmingham)

Miles from Euston

84.20 Flyover GF

RBS

DOWN BIRMINGHAM
UP B'HAM

New Bilton 0.79
Bilton West GF 0.71
Bilton East GF 0.58
Rugby Cement Redland Roof Tiles

RTS

RUGBY and LEAMINGTON LINE

0
Trent Valley Jn 83.18

North Side Up Sidings

LEICESTER SDG

1 2 3 4 5 6 7 8

DOWN GOODS
DOWN FAST
DOWN SLOW
UP & DOWN SLOW
UP FAST
UP GOODS

LEC

Rugby Nth Jn 82.70

FRONT SDG I
ARRIVAL SDG
UP GOODS

LONDON to RUGBY LINE (London & Birmingham)

DOWN MAIN
UP MAIN

DOWN NORTHAMPTON
UP NORTHAMPTON

LEC

HNR

Crick 81.18
Hillmorton 83.53

Rugby PSB (RY) 82.26

RUGBY 82.40

DOWN GOODS
SDG 6B
SDG 5
SDG 6A
DOWN FAST
DOWN SLOW
SDG 2 3
UP FAST
UP GOODS
UP & DN ENGINE
UP SLOW

8 1 6
7 2 3

Clifton Rd Stn Jn
Sdg PARCELS BAY 82.13
SDG 84.46
UP GOODS

Carriage Sidings
Grundig Ltd

BI-DIR

Maintenance & Equipment Depot
S & TE

PETERBOROUGH BRANCH SDG

ROADE AND RUGBY NEW LINE

10B: to Northampton & Roade

B

Miles from Coventry North Jn
5 6 7 8 9

Hawksbury Lane LC 4.71
UGL
Hawksbury La. Up Side Frame GF 5.37

14B: to Coventry

Bedworth
Murco Petroleum (Calor Gas)
BEDWORTH 6.29
Calor Gas Sdgs GF 5.37

94 95 96 97

DOWN COVENTRY
UP COVENTRY

CNN

COVENTRY & NUNEATON LINE

NUNEATON 97.10

9.53
96.68

Nuneaton PSB (NN) 96.65
Cemetery Sidings CE

Nuneaton South Jn 96.02 / 0.02

2 3 4 5

Nuneaton North Jn 10.18 / 97.36

Attleborough Jn 95.49 / 0.58

NWN

South Leicestershire Line
WHITACRE AND NUNEATON LINE

Nuneaton Midland Jn 0.58 / 11.31

LEC
TRENT VALLEY LINE
DOWN MAIN
UP MAIN
DOWN FAST
UP FAST
DOWN SLOW
UP SLOW

DOWN LEICESTER
UP LEICESTER

3B: to Hinckley

18: to Water Orton

Abbey Jn 9.59

NWO
UP B'HAM 99.49 to
DOWN 9.64 to B'HAM
(AJ)

Ashby Jn 97.51

NMA

98 99 100 101 102 103 104 105 106 107 108 109 110

Miles from Euston

Hartshill Sidings CE
South GF 99.37
North GF 99.49

ATHERSTONE 102.23

LEC TRENT VALLEY LINE

DOWN SLOW
DOWN FAST
UP FAST
UP SLOW

River Amber/ Polesworth Viaduct
POLESWORTH 106.39

CE

NN | TH
PSB | SB

18: to Water Orton

11 Miles from Whitacre Junction

TAMWORTH (HIGH LEVEL)

R. Amber/ Tamworth Vdct 23.58

3
Tamworth Low Level SB (TH) 110.12

Temper Stabling CE

4
TAMWORTH (LOW LEVEL) 110.01

18: to Water Orton
12A: to Lichfield

GF 23.44
DOWN UP DBP

18: to Wichnor Jn
BIRMINGHAM and DERBY LINE

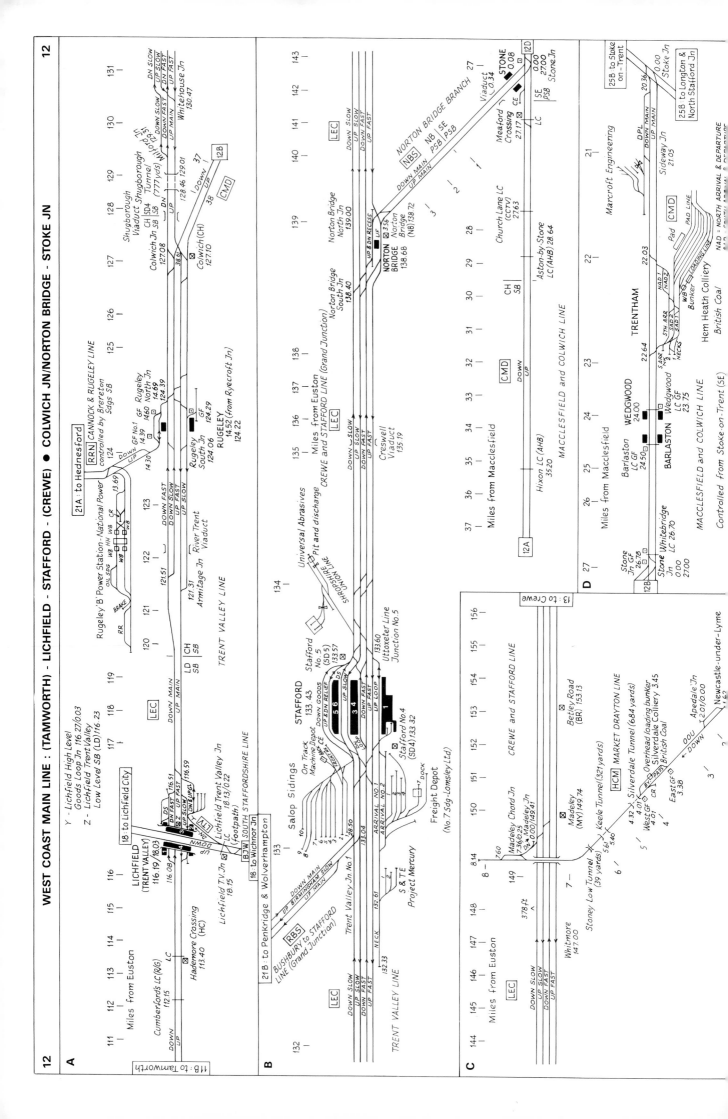

WEST COAST MAIN LINE : (TAMWORTH) - LICHFIELD - STAFFORD - (CREWE) ● COLWICH JN/NORTON BRIDGE - STOKE JN

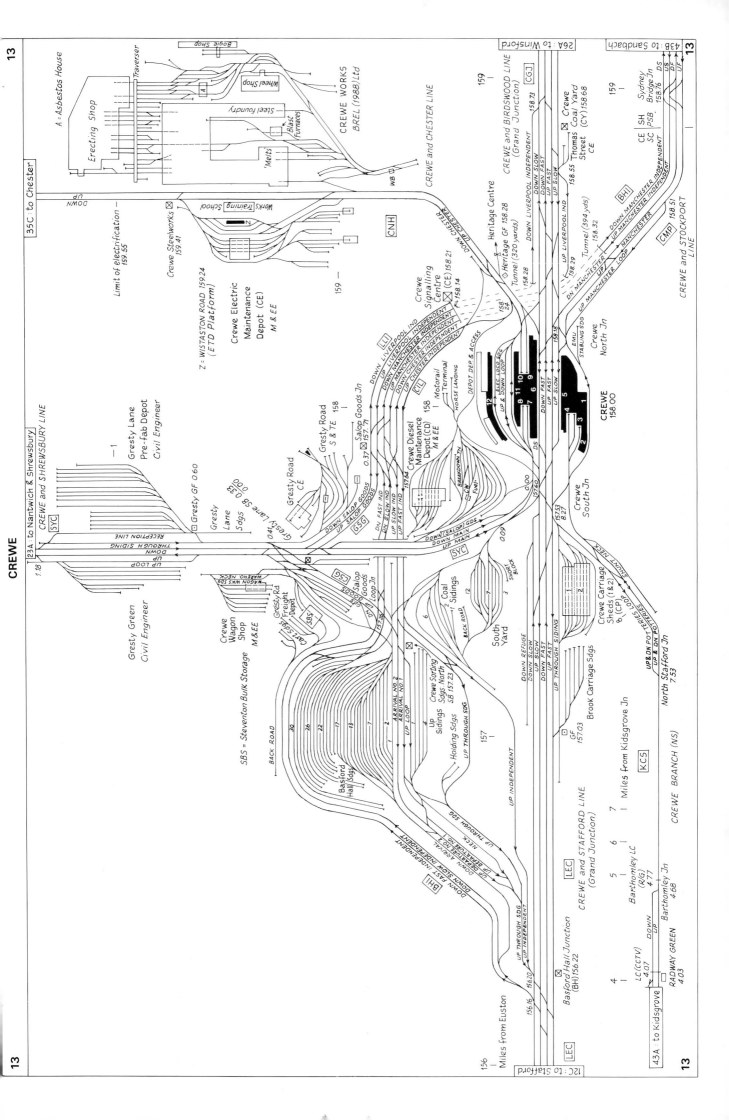

CREWE

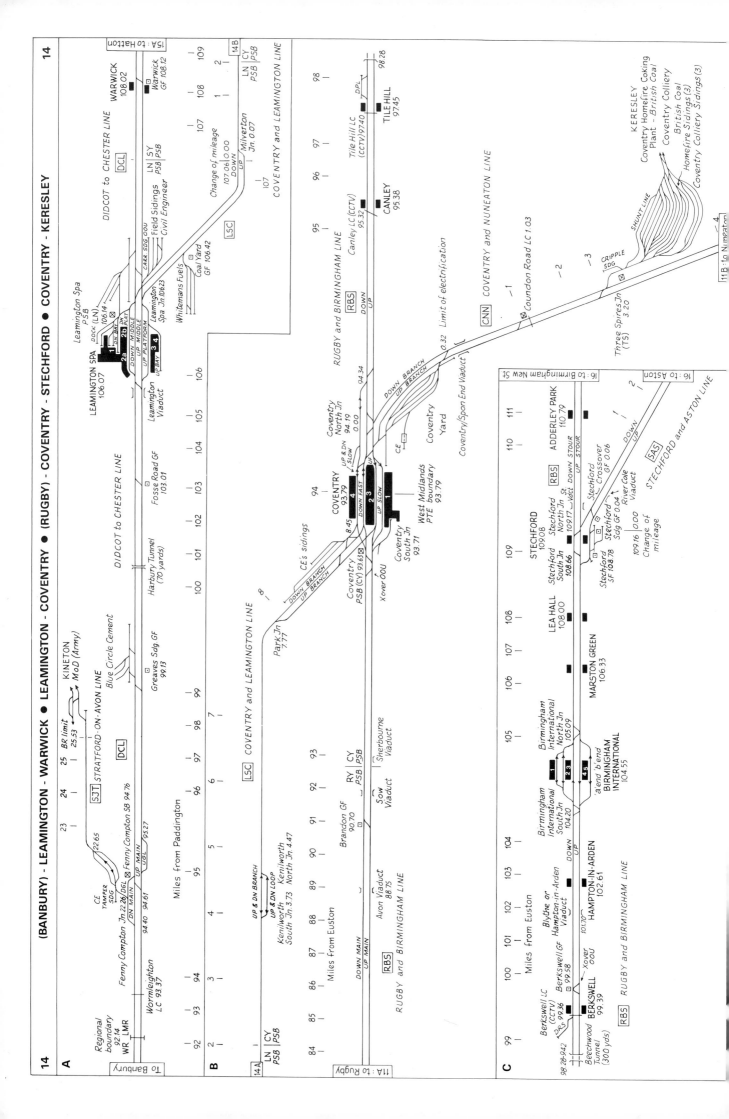

NORTH WARWICK LINE : STRATFORD-UPON-AVON - BIRMINGHAM ● WARWICK - TYSELEY

A

Miles from Honeybourne

NIRU
UP SB
DOWN

8.63

STRATFORD-UPON-AVON 8.77
⊠ Stratford-upon-Avon East SB 9.17
HSA

WILMCOTE 11.49

Bearley Jn 17.69
⊕ 12.72

Edstone LC 14.06

STRATFORD-ON-AVON BRANCH

Bearley West Jn SB (BJ) 12.58/17.61
SD
BEARLEY 13.19

Sillesbourne LC 16.70
WOOTTON WAWEN 15.22

Songar Grancell LC 14.38

BJ SB
SY PSB

⊠ SB 13.34
HENLEY-IN-ARDEN 13.41

BIRMINGHAM and NORTH WARWICK LINE

Wood End Tunnel (173 yds)
WOOD END 8.56

DANZEY 10.43

West Midlands PTE Boundary 5.59
WHITLOCKS END 4.60

Shirley SB (SH) 3.66

SHIRLEY 3.68

THE LAKES 7.50

EARLSWOOD 6.61

WYTHALL 5.59

HALL GREEN 1.29

SPRING ROAD 0.57

YARDLEY WOOD 2.48

SH SB
SY PSB

0.00

DOWN LEAMINGTON
UP LEAMINGTON

12564 12573
Tyseley South Junction

ACOCKS GREEN 125.08

OLTON 124.11

SOLIHULL 122.25

WIDNEY MANOR 120.66

Bentley Heath Crossing 119.43

West Midlands PTE Boundary 118.75

MAT Transport

UP/DNPL
DN MAIN
UP MAIN
SD
DORRIDGE 118.75
P&B

Controlled from Saltley PSB (SY)
DIDCOT and CHESTER LINE
DCL

Miles from Paddington

LAPWORTH 116.31

Lapworth Emergency GF 116.37

112.51/118.18
Hatton North Jn

Hatton West Jn 117.62

HHW
NORTH CURVE

SD   UP DN
18   DN

STRATFORD S CURVE
DOWN
HSA
P&B

Hatton Station Jn
CE (VAU) DPL
HATTON 112.14

CLAVERDON 16.38
— 14
— 15
— 16
— 17

Miles from Honeybourne

WARWICK 108.02
⊠ Warwick GF 108.12

DGL
DOWN
UP

111.02
111

DIDCOT and CHESTER LINE
DCL

BCV

14A : to Leamington Spa

B

Tyseley Traction Maintenance Depot (TS)
M & EE

Birmingham Railway Museum
Standard Gauge Steam Trust

Allen Rowland
(J. Saville Gordon)

WARWICK ROAD

Diesel Shed
Coal Stage
LC
CW
WASH ROAD
Carriage
sdgs
DN THROUGH SIDING
UP THROUGH SIDING
Ramp
Car terminal OOU

Tyseley No 3 GF
Tyseley South Jn
12564 12573

TYSELEY 126.05

DCL

0.00
126.04
3 4   1 2
BCV
126

Tyseley No 1 126.40
GF 126.44

DOWN SLOW
UP SLOW
DOWN FAST
UP FAST

Small Heath South Jn 126.59

Controlled from Saltley PSB (SY)
DIDCOT & CHESTER LINE

Small Heath No 1
GF 12714
SMALL HEATH 127.04
3 4   1 2

127

Small Heath
Coal Concentration Depot
LCP Fuels
Caledonia Yard
6
NO 1 GARDEN RD TRAFFIC NO 1

UP & DOWN SNOWHILL
UP SNOW HILL
DOWN SNOW HILL
DOWN GOODS LOOP
DOWN MAIN
UP MAIN
UP GOODS LOOP
BORDESLEY BRANCH

Bordesley South Jn 127.57

Bordesley Jn 41.44
128.11
Bordesley 128.03

16 : To Saltley & Grand Jn

Miles from Paddington

17E : to Kings Norton
SKN

CAMP HILL LINE
DOWN
UP

GF 12771
—42

Bordesley Viaduct (797 yards)
128.35

New Street Tunnel under 16
See 16

Snow Hill Tunnel (580 yds)

BIRMINGHAM SNOW HILL 129.36
1 2   3 4

12872 12918
BIRMINGHAM MOOR STREET 128.66

DCL
16
129
129.40

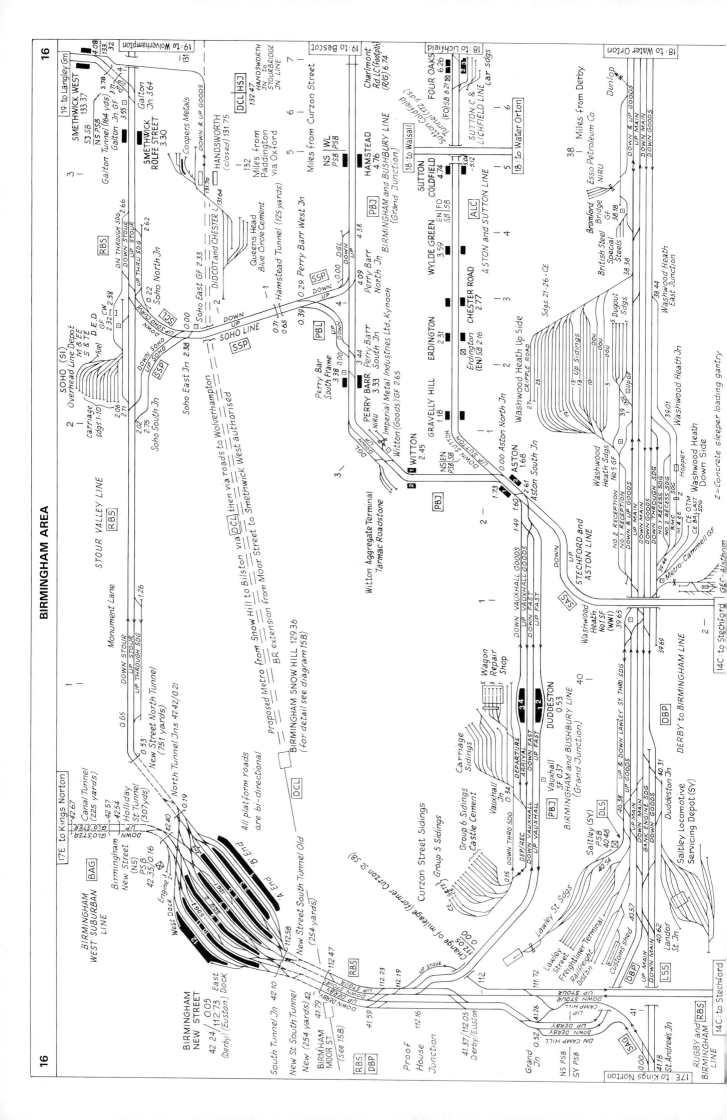

BIRMINGHAM AREA

A GLOUCESTERSHIRE WARWICKSHIRE RAILWAY LTD.

Locomotive sheds
Loco.pit
Loco.pit
TODDINGTON 9.36
9.48
WINCHCOMBE 12.00
Greet Tunnel (693 yds)
1305 12.74
12.57 12.25
Gretton
C & W
10 Miles from Honeybourne East Loop Jn
11
12

B LLANGOLLEN RAILWAY SOCIETY LTD.

SB 00U
LLANGOLLEN 5.40
Miles from Llangollen Line Jn
6
Pentre-felin Sdgs
Pentrefelin Loop
Llangollen Goods Jn
7
Berwyn Viaduct (77 yds)
BERWYN 7.06
Berwyn Loop
Berwyn Tunnel (689 yds)
8
proposed 1991
DEESIDE LOOP 8.62

C BRECON MOUNTAIN RAILWAY CO. LTD.
1' 11¾" gauge

PANT
Loco.shed & works
pits
PONTSTICILL

D GREAT CENTRAL RAILWAY

LEICESTER NORTH
ROTHLEY
Swithland Viaduct
QUORN & WOODHOUSE
LOUGHBOROUGH CENTRAL
WT
Loco shed
SIGNAL BOX HALT

E

16: to Birmingham New Street
16: to Saltley & Grand Jn
41
Miles from Derby via Birmingham New Street
BIRMINGHAM WEST SUBURBAN LINE
Bath Row Tunnel (210 yards) Granville Street Tunnel (225 yds) Canal Tunnel (128 yds)(412-68-72) 42.57-42.67
42.54 42.40
Holliday St. Tunnel (307 yards)
42 41.18 St. Andrews Jn
41.82 11.44
Bordesley Jn 41.44
15B: to Birmingham Snow Hill
15B: to Tyseley
DCL BCV
FIVE WAYS 43.18
43
UNIVERSITY 44.73
BAG
43.61-56 Church Rd SY NS Tunnel PSB(106 yds) PSB
44
Moseley Tunnel (755 yards)
43.54 43.47
Miles from Derby
SKN
BIRMINGHAM and GLOUCESTER LINE
45
SELLY OAK 45.50
Selly Oak Viaduct
BOURNVILLE 46.58
Lifford West Jn 46.36
46
Up Camp Hill
Down Camp Hill
Lifford East Jn 46.11
Lifford Curve UP DOWN
LEL
Pershore Road Tunnel (62 yds) 47.64
47.18
Kings Norton Station Jn 46.59
Kings Norton 46.42
KINGS NORTON GF 47.40
Kings Norton Electrification Depot
NECK ARR & DEP
Kings Norton West GF 47.40
Controlled from Saltley PSB (SY)
BAG
NORTHFIELD 48.12
Longbridge East
North Works
North Sdg GF 0.00
UP SLOW
UP FAST
DOWN FAST
DOWN SLOW
Halesowen Jn
LONGBRIDGE 49.12
West Midlands PTE boundary
West Sidings
LONGBRIDGE and HALESOWEN BRANCH
6 5 1
0.70 0.60
LONGBRIDGE Austin Rover
South Works
DMU REV.SDG
0.26
SHUNT LINE 1
RECEPTION LINE 1
ARR/DEP
UP SDG 1
Halesowen Up Slow Jn 49.33
49.21
Cofton Austin Rover Cofton Sdg GF 50.08
Railway GF
DOWN MAIN
UP MAIN
50.34
DOWN GOODS
UP GOODS
BIRMINGHAM and GLOUCESTER LINE
BAG
G SY PSB PSB
Blackwell Summit (564 ft)
WR < LMR
Regional boundary 52.40
Miles from Derby via Camp Hill Line
BARNT GREEN 51.67
Barnt Green Jn 51.58
52.11
BAG
BEA BARNT GREEN, EVESHAM and MALVERN LINE
ALVECHURCH 53.47
53
54
55
REDDITCH 56.61
56

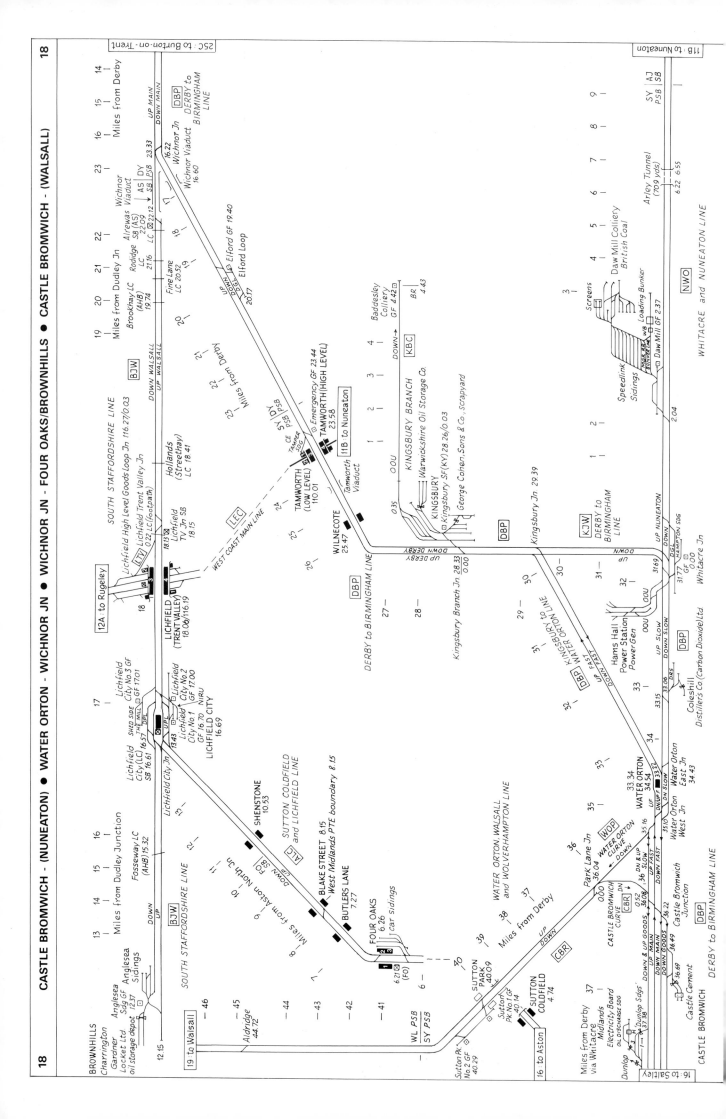

WEST MIDLANDS : SMETHWICK, DUDLEY, BESCOT, WALSALL AND WOLVERHAMPTON

20C : to Stourbridge Junction

HANDSWORTH JN. to STOURBRIDGE JN. LINE

20C : to Stourbridge Junction

Round Oak North GF 145.71

OXFORD, WORCESTER and WOLVERHAMPTON LINE

Miles from Paddington via Worcester

Miles from Paddington via Snow Hill

GSJ

Langley Gn. West LC (CCTV) 135.60
135.09
135 —
146 —
147 —
148 —

Albright & Wilson

OLDBURY BRANCH

ICI —
(LG) 134.46
134.49
134.40
134.04 GDS

Rood End Yard

British Industrial Plastics

134 —
133 —

SMETHWICK WEST
133.37
133.32

RBS

4.08/133.32

HSJ
16: to Handsworth

NS SJ PSB SB

Galton Jn
GF 3.55

Galton Tnl. (164 yds)
3.64
3.71.78

16: to Birmingham New St.

DN STOURBRIDGE
UP STOURBRIDGE
UP/DN GDS

5
5.28
SANDWELL & DUDLEY

5.76

Gulf Oil

Albion

Great Bridge

Great Bridge Steel Terminal

Change of mileage (Dudley Jn)
DUDLEY PORT
7.29
7.35
7.43

DPJ
OWW

147.37
147.79
148.00
148.20

Dudley Tunnel (944 yards)

Watery La SB & LC
7.75
CE LC

DN GDS
DN MAIN
UP MAIN
UP GOODS

DOWN STOUR
UP STOUR

SOUTH STAFFORDSHIRE LINE

LC 2.23
2.04
— 2

TIPTON
8.16
TIPTON
8.16

Ocker Hill Power Station National Power

Eagle Crossing 2.21

Coal Plant

COSELEY
9.46

STOUR VALLEY LINE

Miles from Birmingham New Street

9
10
11
12
13

DOWN STOUR
UP STOUR

MONMORE GREEN

British Oxygen Co Ltd

Birmingham Canal

11.62
11.71

Wolverhampton (Walsall Street) Steel Terminal
140.49
140.79
141.19

Loading shed

BILSTON
138.54
J. Norton & Sons

13.8
138

Wednesbury Sdgs Steel Terminal

Wednesbury Central Jn
136.77
137
0.31

NIRU — Miles from Paddington via Oxford

WST DCL
DIDCOT & CHESTER LINE

Low Level

Engineering Sdgs

Cripples Sdgs

Exchange Sdgs

CE Not in regular use

136.54
3.40
3.22
3.27
0.00

Brunswick Down Sdgs (1-6 not in regular use)

Wednesbury Town Jn 3.27
Wednesbury SB (WY) 3.26

Proposed Birmingham Snow Hill–Bilston–Wolverhampton Metro

NS WN PSB PSB

WOLVERHAMPTON
West Midlands PTE boundary
1275
PSB 1269

CE —
13
21B
RBS

21B : to Penkridge

15
14

Wednesfield Road Railstore - CE

Heath Town Jn
53.18-Miles from Derby
53 — via Water Orton
5279

WATER ORTON, WALSALL and WOLVERHAMPTON LINE

13.73
13.65

Wednesfield Heath Tunnel (179 yards)

DOWN BRANCH
UP BRANCH
Xover OOJ
1.59 U 2 & DN GOODS
12.60

PORTOBELLO LOOP
1.29
53.24

PORTOBELLO & HEATH TOWN JN. LINE

DOWN
PORTOBELLO

0.04

DJW

13

Portobello Junction
0.04

Noose Lane LC (CCTV)
12.64
12.47

PBJ

BIRMINGHAM and BUSHBURY LINE

Miles from Curzon Street

WL PSB / WN PSB

Darlaston GF 10.01
9.65

Darlaston Junction
0.15
0.00

UP DARLASTON
DOWN DARLASTON

WDJ

WL SB
WY SB

10
11

18 : to Water Orton
18
19

WALSALL and CANNOCK LINE

21A : to Bloxwich

PRN

Change of mileage 6.79 000

DOWN CANNOCK
UP CANNOCK

CBR

WATER ORTON, WALSALL and WOLVERHAMPTON LINE

UP WATER ORTON
DOWN WATER ORTON

6.70
6.79 000
47

Ryecroft Jn
47.54

BJW
STH STAFFORDSHIRE LINE

Park Street Tunnel (143 yards)

Permanent Way Depot

Per Way Yard
CE

Pleck Jn GF
5.60
1.16
5.44

Walsall PSB (WL) 5.42

WALSALL
6.29
6.34
6.40
6.40
6.18

Walsall North Jn

Walsall South Jn
Tasker Street

Brook Sdg

Midland Yard

DOWN SLOW
DOWN FAST
UP SLOW
UP FAST

DOWN MAIN
UP MAIN

CE limit of electrification

6

Bescot Curve Jn
0.00/4.73 (limit of elect.)
0.61

DN DUDLEY
UP DUDLEY

DPJ

UP WEDNESBURY CURVE
DN WEDNESBURY CURVE

WGL

DOWN BESCOT
UP BESCOT

PLECK CURVE

BJW

Bescot Jn
0.01

Bescot Traction Maintenance Depot (BS)

BESCOT STADIUM
8.47

BESCOT YARD

Inwards Arrival Line

Down Storage Sidings

Down Sorting Sdgs

Up & Dn Reception Sdgs
Bescot Dn Wr (BT)
Dn Local Sdg
Engine Sdgs
ENGINE LOCAL LINE

THRO' SDG
SHUNTING

Up & Dn Goods
Up Main
Down Main

Engine Reception Sdgs

Holding Sidings

Up Sorting Sidings

Up Local Sorting Sidings

Marcroft Engineering

Newton Jn
7.59
7.48
TAME BRIDGE

SHUNTING NECK

PBJ
WL PSB

BIRMINGHAM and BUSHBURY JN. LINE (Grand Junction)

16 : to Aston

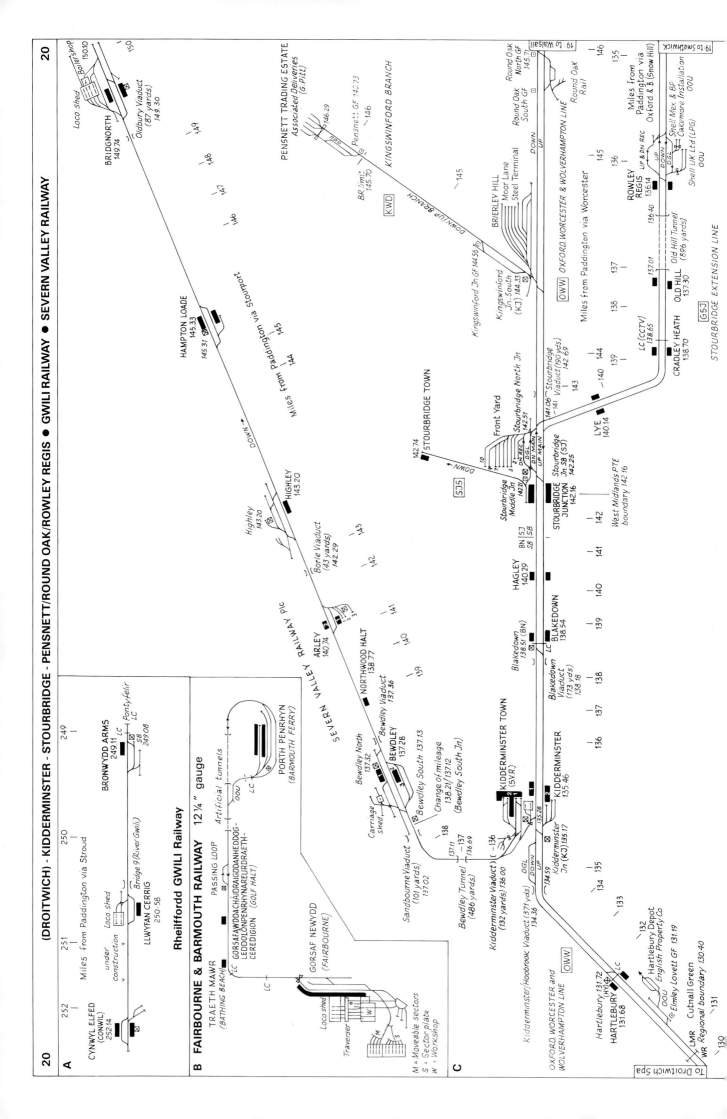

20

(DROITWICH) - KIDDERMINSTER - STOURBRIDGE - PENSNETT/ROUND OAK/ROWLEY REGIS ● GWILI RAILWAY ● SEVERN VALLEY RAILWAY

20

(WALSALL) - CANNOCK - (RUGELEY) ● (WOLVERHAMPTON) - COSFORD - (TELFORD) ● IRONBRIDGE BRANCH

A

Miles from Ryecroft Junction

CANNOCK and RUGELEY LINE

CANNOCK BRANCH

Imperial Smelting Corpn

Essington Wood Opencast 4
British Coal

Bloxwich (BH) 2·06

Bloxwich SB

THOMAS SDG
GF
LC 2·22
WB

BLOXWICH 2·32

BLOXWICH NORTH 3·01

3·41
3·61
MGR R&R
LOADING SDG Bunker
CRIPPLE SDG
RECEPTION 2

WYRLEY & CHESLYN HAY 5·67

LANDYWOOD 5·12

Mid Cannock Colliery GF 6·30

Mid Cannock Opencast
British Coal OOU

CANNOCK 7·16

IND. COAL FUEL
IND. Y COAL REC
MGR LOADING
WB Z
MGR R&R
CR

Y = Industrial Coal Bunker
Z = Merry-go-round Coal Bunker

RRN

DOWN
UP

HEDNESFORD 9·05

Hednesford SB 9·12

Crossover OOU

Moors Gorse LC

Lea Hall 13·34 13·53 13·69

to Rugeley 'B' Power Stn.

12A: to Rugeley

Reception Sidings 12A

Lea Hall Colliery
British Coal

Brereton Sidings 13·25

Departure
Screens
28

12B: to Stafford

Trent Valley Jn No. 1 28·50

DOWN MAIN
UP MAIN
UP BIRMINGHAM SLW
27·55
Rickerscote

DOWN
UP

LEC

12B: to Rugeley

B

Miles from Birmingham (Curzon Street Signal Box) via Bescot

BUSHBURY to STAFFORD LINE (Grand Junction)

OY SB
WN PSB

142·79
143·02
143·14
143·07
102 Oxley (Stafford Rd Jn)

VICTORIA BASIN BRANCH 143·52

WS
STOUR VALLEY LINE
DOWN
UP SB
WN PSB
OY SB

19: to Wolverhampton

Bushbury Viaduct
Bushbury Jn 14·43

not electrified

OXC

14
15·23
15·32
DGL
DOWN
UP
Bushbury/Oxley Jn

000
Wolverhampton North Jn

RBS

13·32

BIRMINGHAM and BUSHBURY LINE

OXLEY CHORD
DOWN
UP

PBJ

former

Croda Synthetic Chemicals
UGL 20·18
Four Ashes Hopper No. 1 GF 1972

Littleton Colliery SF 22·74

Littleton Colliery
British Coal
THRO
In
Out
Bunker
1
2

WN PSB
SD4 SB

PENKRIDGE 23·32

Penkridge Viaduct

RBS

26
27
28

C

DIDCOT and CHESTER LINE

Miles from Paddington via Oxford and Birmingham Snow Hill

Oxley (Stafford Rd Jn)
Change of mileage
142·79 | 143·02

OXLEY CHORD
DN UP
DOWN
UP
21B: to Bescot

Oxley (OY) 143·14
Oxley Viaduct (188 yds) 143·07

WN PSB
OY SB

Carriage Washing Sdgs
CW
DGL
DOWN
UP
UGL
DGL

OXLEY CARRIAGE SIDINGS (OY)

Carriage shed
17
18
16
15
12
11
8
5
1
2

143·65
Limit of electrification

BILBROOK 145·66

CODSALL 146·41
Codsall (CL) 146·26

WSJ

Greggs LC 148·45

ALBRIGHTON 149·38

COSFORD 150·69
Cosford 151·07

DOWN
UGL
DGL
UP

Tamper Sdg-CE

Ruckley Viaduct (90 yds) 152·09

SHIFNAL 154·24
Shifnal Viaduct (194 yds) 154·29

156·19

Madeley Jn (MY) 156·26

Madeley South Jn 156·51

MADELEY BRANCH
ICW

DRS
DOWN
UP

21D

22A: to Telford

D

MADELEY BRANCH

KETLEY BRANCH

Madeley South Jn 156·51

21C

Lightmoor Junction
MADELEY 159·10
160·15 | 162·25
162·21

Coalbrookdale Viaduct (264 yards) 161·25

Clunes LC 160·55

MJI

DOWN
UP

Royal Albert Bridge

IRONBRIDGE GORGE (Seasonal, temporary)

OIL SDG
SD
CR

End of running line 160·03

No. 2 RECEPTION WB
No. 1 RECEPTION
No. 2 DEPARTURE
No. 1 DEPARTURE
HH WB

160·16

IRONBRIDGE POWER STATION
National Power

159·25

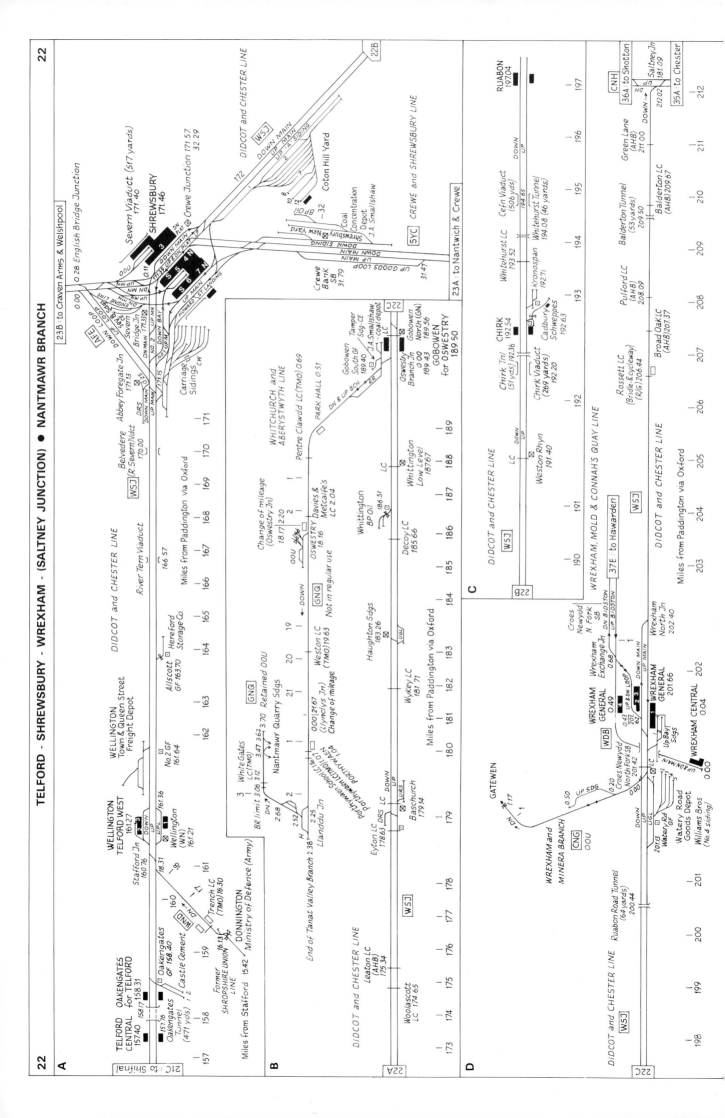

(SHREWSBURY) - WHITCHURCH - (CREWE) ● SHREWSBURY & HEREFORD LINE ● CAMBRIAN LINES : (SHREWSBURY) - ABERYSTWYTH ● VALE OF RHEIDOL RLY.

A

13 : to Crewe

1.18

Harlescott Crossing 30.29
LC

Willaston LC (CCTV) 2.41
Nantwich Emergency GF 4.01
Nantwich Emergency GF 3.46
Nantwich LC (AHB) 4.19
NANTWICH LC 4.14

Limit of electrification 1.41

Shrewbridge LC (AHB) 4.32

Reeds Farm LC 6.51

Marley Green LC 10.10
WRENBURY 8.48
Wrenbury 8.52
Marley Green Emergency Trailing Crossover GF 10.17
Marley Green Emergency Facing Crossover GF 10.14

Brick Kiln Lane LC 12.49

Whitchurch 13.35
Darlington's LC 14.32
WHITCHURCH 13.44

DOWN
UP

Prees 18.39
PREES 18.36

WEM 21.55
Wem 21.52
Wem LC
Tilley LC 22.50
DRS
Wem Emergency Facing Crossover GF 21.72
Wem Emergency Trailing Crossover GF 21.76

YORTON 25.14

Miles from Crewe South Junction

CREWE and SHREWSBURY LINE

22A : to Shrewsbury

Regional boundary
WR LMR
18.10

To Craven Arms

B

Coleham Sidings
CE
English Bridge Jn

UP MAIN
DOWN MAIN

Abbey 0.00
Abbey Viaduct 0.31
Sutton Bridge Jn SB 0.65 (SB)
(Token Exchange Point)
SHREWSBURY
22A : to Shrewsbury
0.28

REFUGE SDG
SBA
DOWN
SD
0.00
0.68
UP MAIN
DOWN MAIN
UP GOODS MAIN
DN GOODS LOOP

Coleham Shelf Sidings

Sutton Bridge GF 1.07

23C
23B

1.31

SHREWSBURY to HEREFORD LINE

SHL

SYC

Micklewood LC 7.66

Leebotwood LC 8.43

Heather Brae LC 10.14

Stretton LC 11.38

CHURCH STRETTON 12.63
Church Stretton 12.54
URS
UP
DOWN
613ft

Woodland LC 14.66

Marsh Brook 15.29

Hopper
GF 3.78
Bayston Hill
Tarmac

GF 6.09
Dorrington 6.25
DRS

C

Harwood LC 4.09

Stretton Heath LC (AOCL) 8.76

23B
SBA

UP LP
DU 10.10
Westbury LC (AOCL) 10.25
10.30

Plas-y-Court LC (AOCL) 12.41

Buttington 31.20 16.19
Change of mileage 32.27
Buttington LC (AOCL) 32.27

Miles from Sutton Bridge Jn

Parry Green LC Smiths Lower Cefn LC 16.00

Buttington Gates Flood Viaduct (38 yds)

Welshpool GF 33.70
WELSHPOOL 33.78
UP DN LOOP
34.10
34.55

Glanrafon Viaduct (31 yds)

Fron LC 36.40

Kilkewydd Viaduct (74 yds)

Forden LC (AOCL) 38.20

Rhydwhimen LC (R/G) 39.70

MONTGOMERY LC (R/G) 40.18

Abermule LC (AOCL) 43.63

Miles from Whitchurch via Oswestry

Controlled by RETB from MH (* = Token Exchange Point)

D

Cilgwrgan LC (R/G) 45.22

MH | SB
SB | SB

NEWTOWN 47.56
UL
4779
TROLLEY SDG 47.79
DN BAY SDG
Newtown GF 47.58
DL 47.47

Doughtys Viaduct (62 yds)

Llanidloes Rd LC 52.70
GF 53.31
CAERSWS (CS)

Maesmawr Accommodation LC 52.42

Weig Lane LC (AOCL) 54.26

River Severn Viaduct (66 yds)

Carno LC (AOCL) 59.17
Sarn LC 59.40

Bullock (Oerffrwyd) LC 57.34

Talerddig GF 61.11
UL
DL
61.34 61.12

Sarn Pile Viaduct (19 yds)

Village Viaduct (18 yds)

Caetwpa LC 63.13

Old Chapel LC (R/G) 63.34

Llanbrynmair LC (R/G) 64.58

Cemmes Road LC (R/G) 70.05

Llanbadarn LC (ABCL) 94.56

Miles from Whitchurch via Oswestry

UP & DOWN SHREWSBURY

SBA

SHREWSBURY and WELSHPOOL LINE
WHITCHURCH and ABERYSTWYTH LINE

Controlled by RETB from MH (* = Token Exchange Point)

E

Machynlleth (MH)
MACHYNLLETH 75.04
UP DN SHREWSBURY
75.11
75.21
TANK SDG 74.74
(MN)
AB
AB = ABERYSTWYTH SIDING
UP & DN SHREWSBURY

WHITCHURCH and ABERYSTWYTH LINE

24A : to Tywyn

Dovey Jn 78.60
DOVEY JUNCTION 79.06
UP & DN ABERYSTWYTH
Track Circuit Block System
UP & DN DOVEY

Cottage Pie Viaduct (24 yds)

RHIWFRON 10.70
RHEIDOL FALLS 9.22

VALE OF RHEIDOL RAILWAY (11'11½" gauge)
(Owned by Brecon Mountain Rly.)

DEVIL'S BRIDGE
GF 11.65
680' above sea level
11.72

SBA
UP & DN ABERYSTWYTH

Aberlieri Ynyslas LC (AHB) 86.04
BORTH 87.27
Borth Capel Soar LC 87.59 (AOCL)

Leri Viaduct (49 yards)

CAPEL BANGOR 4.48
Capel Bangor LC 4.54

NANTYRONEN 6.58
Nantyronen LC 6.55

ABERFFRWD 7.53
Aberffrwd LC 7.55

Trer'ddol River Viaduct (28 yards)

Llandre Vicarage 90.02
Llandre LC (AOCL) 89.58

Capel Bangor

DOWN

GLANRAFON 2.26
Glanrafon LC (AOCL)

New Glanyrafon LC 2.02

Miles from Whitchurch via Oswestry

Aberystwyth - Dovey Jn. controlled by RETB from MH
(* = Token Exchange Point)

Controlled by RETB from MH (* = Token Exchange Point)

LLANBADARN 1.14
Llanbadarn LC (AOCL)

Aberystwyth Oil Distributors

ABERYSTWYTH 95.60
Aberystwyth No.1 GF 95.30
0.15
Up Sdgs
UP & DOWN
WAGON SDG
Platforms 4 & 5 are OOU
SDG 1
SDG 2 GF 95.56
SDG 3
Vale of Rheidol GF 0.25

V = CARRIAGE OR LONG SDG
X = BACK THROUGH
Y = MIDDLE OR CROSSOVER ROAD
Z = PIT ROAD

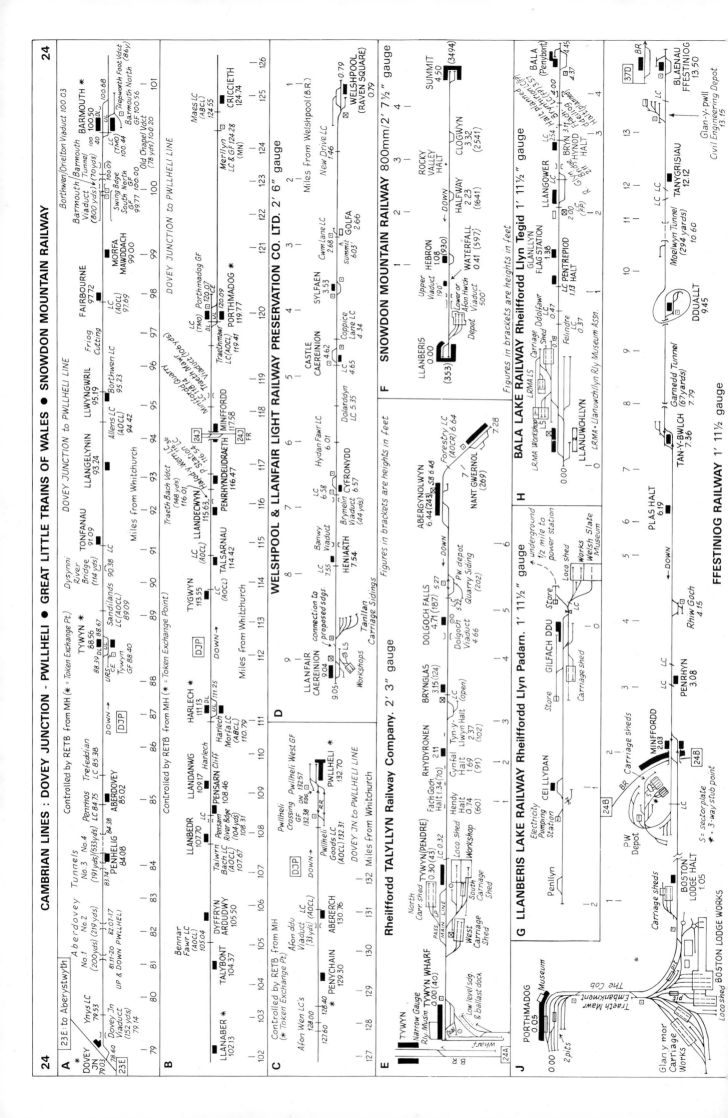

CAMBRIAN LINES : DOVEY JUNCTION - PWLLHELI ● GREAT LITTLE TRAINS OF WALES ● SNOWDON MOUNTAIN RAILWAY

A

FOXFIELD LIGHT RAILWAY SOCIETY LTD.

BLYTHE BRIDGE
(CAVERSWALL ROAD)

FOXFIELD COLLIERY

DILHORNE PARK
LC

Loco. Shed & Museum

Running shed

BLYTHE BRIDGE

25B

B.R.

LC

Caldon Low
GF
7.62

Caldon Low
GF
8.03

RR

CALDON LOW

DOWN →
8

WATERHOUSES BRANCH

SCQ

WB   LS
10.08

OAKAMOOR

WB
10.21

UP
DOWN

Westons Lane LC (AHB) 13.71
Stableshams LC 14.50
Bramshall LC (AHB) 13.2

DERBY LINE

NSS

CVL

Miles from Uttoxeter
CHURNET VALLEY LINE

Boltons Sdg
LC 12.40

Leigh LC
10.24

Upper Leigh LC
9.57

Newton LC
(Farm) 7.61

Cresswell
LC (AHB)
6.76

Stallington
LC (CCTV-Caverswall)
5.42

LC (CCTV)
5.19

BLYTHE BRIDGE
5.23

Caverswall
4.20   UGL

25A

DGL   UP
DOWN
LC

Daggdale LC 11.59
Brandwids LC 11.72
B. Heaths LC 8.21

NOT IN REGULAR USE

15   14   13   12   11   10   9   8   7   6   5

Leek Brook Jn SB 6.58/17.50
Leek Brook Jn
17.57

6.65/0.00
0.08

Cheddleton Tunnel
(531 yards)
17.28

Cheddleton
LC (TMO) 16.45
16.43

CHEDDLETON
17.04 — 17

16

DOWN
UP
6.37

25C

SCQ

LEEK LINE

NOT IN REGULAR USE

Stockton Brook Tunnel
(72 yds)
2.09—2.12

Endon LC (AOCL)
3.11

Change of mileage

Abbey LC (TMO) 3.20

BIDDULPH VALLEY LINE

1   2   3   4   5   6

Apesford
LC 3.20

LC
1.54

LC
3.69

(Milton Jn) 0.00
3.51

B

MACCLESFIELD and COLWICH LINE

Cockshute Sdg

GF North Western Yard
9.44

Cockshute Sdgs

Newcastle Jn
19.35

Cliffe Vale Vdct
19.19

Cliff Vale
English China Clay

Shelton Wharf

ETRURIA
18.64

Miles from Macclesfield

LC
19.14

25B

Fenton Manor Tunnel (106 yds)

UP DERBY
DOWN DERBY

UP MAIN
DN MAIN

Stoke Jn
20.36

Seven Arches
Vdct. 20.20

STOKE-ON-TRENT
20.33
19.78

Stoke on TPSB
19.61 (SE)

Stoke North Jn
19.61

Glebe
St. Jn
20.08

Stoke
St. Jn

12D: to Wedgwood

1

LONGTON
1.71

Foley Crossing Vdct Tunnel
1.56

Longton Meir
Vdct Tunnel
(814 yds)
1.75

3.12   3.49

CMD

BAY

UPL

UP MN
L & UP MN

SAG 0.00
BRDN 20.33
0.00
0.63
0.68

UP BDN THROUGH

UP THROUGH
DOWN THROUGH

1   2   3   4

5   6   7   8   9   10   11   12   13   14   15

16   17   18   19   20

Miles from Macclesfield

43A: to Longport

C

Miles from Derby

UTTOXETER
16.29
16

Hockley LC (CCTV)
Uttoxeter bridge St. LC 16.00
Uttoxeter SB 16.17
16.18

DBP

DGL

DOWN
UP

DERBY to BIRMINGHAM LINE

UP MAIN
DOWN MAIN
UP THROUGH SDG
DOWN THROUGH SDG

Branston Jn
12.15
12.19

Branston
GF 12.71.13

BIRMINGHAM CURVE

Birmingham
Curve Jn
12.60

Cambridge
St. LC 12.60

M. St.
GF
11.00

Mosley St Sdgs

CE

BCJ

KSL

BURTON ON TRENT
10.67

Leicester Jn
11.17
12.70.00

DP Leicester G

7B: to Coalville

LEICESTER and BURTON LINE

18: to Wichnor Jn & Tamworth

Dovefields
LC (R/G)
18.78
19.62

MARCHINGTON 18.78

Sudbury
20.67

LC

Sudbury Vdct
21.16

Scropton
22.53

Marston LC
(AHB)
25.20

Tutbury Crossing
24.13

TUTBURY & HATTON
24.13

LC

Cargo Bonding

MGR Depot - C&W

New Wetmore Sdgs

DEP
DEP
DEP

UP GOODS
UP MAIN
DOWN MAIN
DOWN GOODS
ARR

West Yard

East Yard

Clay Mills Jn LC
(CCTV) 8.54

10.25

Controlled from Derby (DY)

NSS

Miles from Stoke Jn

Findern LC (AHB) 29.49

Willington LC (AHB)
30.40

North Stafford Jn
30.10

Stenson LC
4.16

Stenson Jn
4.50
132.12

UP Chellaston
DN Chellaston

132.05

6C: to Sheet Stores Jn

STENSON BRANCH

DBP

Willington Power Station
National Power

HOPPER LINE
ARR

CR

WB   HS
WB   WS

DEP

Eggington LC
(AHB) 27.50

Eggington Jn
(EN) 26.69
26.67

Hilton LC 27.08

Hilton
Ministry of Defence (Army)

Ramp
Ramp

153.52
153.29

28

27

DERBY LINE

Miles from Stoke Jn

DOWN STOKE
UP STOKE

MJS

(from 130.09 St. Pancras)

Sinfin No.3 GF
130.31

Sinfin No.2 GF
130.56

Sinfin No.1 GF
130.69

SINFIN NORTH
130.73

SINFIN CENTRAL 130.37

Rolls Royce Ltd
130.27

S & T Sdg
GF 0.27

Sunny Hill
2.40

Melbourne Jn 131.15/1.22
131.21

Melbourne LC 131.31/1.32

RAMSLINE HALT

48: to Derby

DERBY to MELBOURNE LINE

DERBY TO BIRMINGHAM LINE

UP MAIN WEST
DN MAIN W
DN MN W
DN GOODS W
DN GOODS W

UGL

L.8
N.W.
0.75

—131

208 UP MAIN
UP MAIN
DOWN MAIN

ND

25

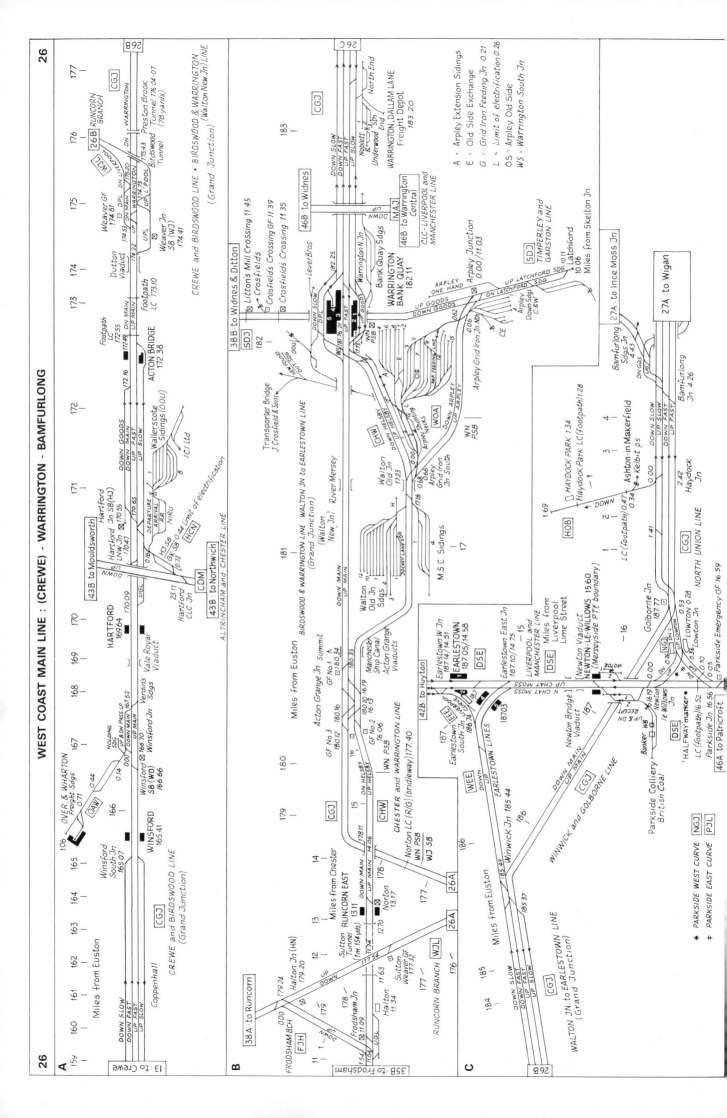

WEST COAST MAIN LINE : (CREWE) - WARRINGTON - BAMFURLONG

WEST COAST MAIN LINE : BAMFURLONG - WIGAN - PRESTON ● WIGAN - ORRELL

42A : to Southport
DOWN SOUTHPORT LINE
Miles from Manchester Vict.
WIGAN and SOUTHPORT LINE
UP SOUTHPORT
WBS
WBS
Miles from Newton-le-Willows Jn
CGJ
27B
Blainscough Emergency GF 12.14
Blainscough GF
WN | PN | PSB
Standish LC (footpath) 9.34
Boars Head GFs No.2 No.1 8.53 8.58
Wigan Carriage Sdgs
DOWN MAIN | UP MAIN
Beggars Walk LC (footpath) 8.06

Lancashire Tar Distillers (Larfina)
Petrofina
PORT OF PRESTON AUTHORITY
Preston Docks
Exchange Sdgs

49A : to Kirkham
28A : to Lancaster
CGJ
Preston PSB (PN)
Holding Sdgs
DOWN BLACKPOOL
UP BLACKPOOL
PBN
Preston Fylde Jn 0.48
Deepdale Jn 0.00/1.31
Deepdale Tunnels No.1 (162 yards) No.2 (272 yards) No.3 (384 yards)
DOWN
Mill St Skeffington Rd LC (TMO)
0.23
SHUNTING LINE
0.41
0.31
0.34
0.46
0.47
0.65
Dock St. 0.03
Dock St. Sdgs CE
PRESTON and LONGRIDGE LINE
PDB
Preston (Deepdale) CCD
National Fuel Distributors
Blue Circle Cement
1.53

Strand Road LC 0.42
Strand Road GF 0.44
PSR PRESTON : RIBBLE BCH
Strand Road GF 0.43
DOWN
Christian Road 0.28
Fishergate Tunnel (140 yards) 0.27
Christian Road Gds 0.22
11
North Union Yard
RIBBLE BCH
2.41(41.00)
PRESTON : RIBBLE BCH
DG
UG
Parcel Carriage Sdgs
Parcel platform
1b 1 2 a
3c b3 a
4c b4 a
b 5 6 a
GOODS LOOP
US/DS
UP FAST
DOWN FAST
DOWN THROUGH
UP THROUGH
PRESTON 21.57/0.00 North Jn
21.39
Preston Preston South Jn

PSS – PARCEL SIDING SOUTH
PSN – PARCEL SIDING NORTH

Adam Viaduct
UP LIVERPOOL
DOWN LIVERPOOL
LOSTOCK JN. to PEMBERTON LINE
WKL
Wigan Wallgate 18.09
Wigan Wallgate 18.04
(WW)
Wigan North Jn
WIGAN WALLGATE Greater Manchester PTE boundary 17.72
WIGAN NORTH WESTERN 6.47
5 6
3 4
2 1
DOWN PASSENGER LOOP
DOWN THROUGH
UP THRO
UP PASS
NW Parcels
WN | WW PSB SB
6.60
6.33 Wigan Station Jn 17.44
Wigan South Jn
6.10
INCE 16.70
48A : to Hindley
DOWN HINDLEY
UP HINDLEY
WBS LOSTOCK JN to PEMBERTON LINE

PEMBERTON 19.23
Winstanley FPLC 19.70
Pemberton Tunnel (40 yds)
19.29–19.27 1908 19.48 Change of mileage (Pemberton Jn)
19
ORRELL (Gtr Man. PTE bay) 20.77
20
21
41A : to Kirkby

Ribble Viaduct
Preston Ribble Jn 21.09
NORTH UNION LINE

Canal Sidings Civil Engineer
Springs Branch Jn No.2 Jn
Springs Branch North Sidings
12.54 Springs Branch Jn DS
5.57
5.25
5.18
Springs Branch No.1 Jn
DOWN SLOW | UP SLOW | DOWN FAST | UP FAST | DOWN MAIN | UP MAIN | DOWN GOODS | UP GOODS
CGJ
NORTH UNION LINE
Wigan. Ince Moss Tip CE
Wigan. Springs Branch TMD (SP) M & EE
1 2 3 4 5
8 9 10 12
6
UP ST HELENS
DOWN ST HELENS

LANCASHIRE UNION LINE
42B : to St.Helens
SBH
12 12
12.10
Ince Moss Jn 0.78
0.68
INCE MOSS GOODS LINES
IMG
Limit of electrification
Bamfurlong Springs Branch 0.00
BAMFURLONG GOODS LINES
Bamfurlong Sdgs M & EE
1.25
SBH
Bamfurlong Springs Branch 000
Bickershaw LC 1.66
BIK
Bickershaw Colliery British Coal
Loading Bunker
Bolton House Road LC
WB | CR
DOWN

Bamfurlong Sidings Jn 0.18
DN GOODS 4.43
0.30
DOWN SLOW | UP SLOW | DOWN FAST | UP FAST | DOWN MAIN | UP MAIN
CGJ
Bamfurlong Jn 4.26

26C : to Warrington Bank Quay & Newton-le-Willows

B
27A
27C
CGJ
Balshaw Lane Jn 14.18
16.22 Euston Jn 25.31
25.17
48A : to Charley
DAF
18.77
0.00 Farington Jn
C
Viaduct
13 14 15 16 17 18 19
DOWN MAIN | UP MAIN | DOWN SLOW | UP SLOW | DOWN FAST | UP FAST
CGJ
LEYLAND 17.54
27B

49C : to Ormskirk
WALTON JN. to PRESTON LINE (Farington Curve)
FCO
Farington Curve Emergency GF
0.06/25.64
0.00
Farington Curve Jn 20.08
DOWN GOODS | UP GOODS | DOWN SLOW | UP SLOW | DOWN FAST | UP FAST
Skew Bridge Jn 20.41
NORTH UNION LINE

WALTON JN. to PRESTON LINE (Farington Curve) LINE
LOSTOCK HALL CONNECTING LINE
FHR
LOSTOCK HALL 1.20
0.75
OOU
DOWN | UP
LOSTOCK HALL LINES (Farington Old Curve)
LHL
1.42 Lostock Hall Jn
0.77
limit of electrification
33A : to Blackburn

27 27

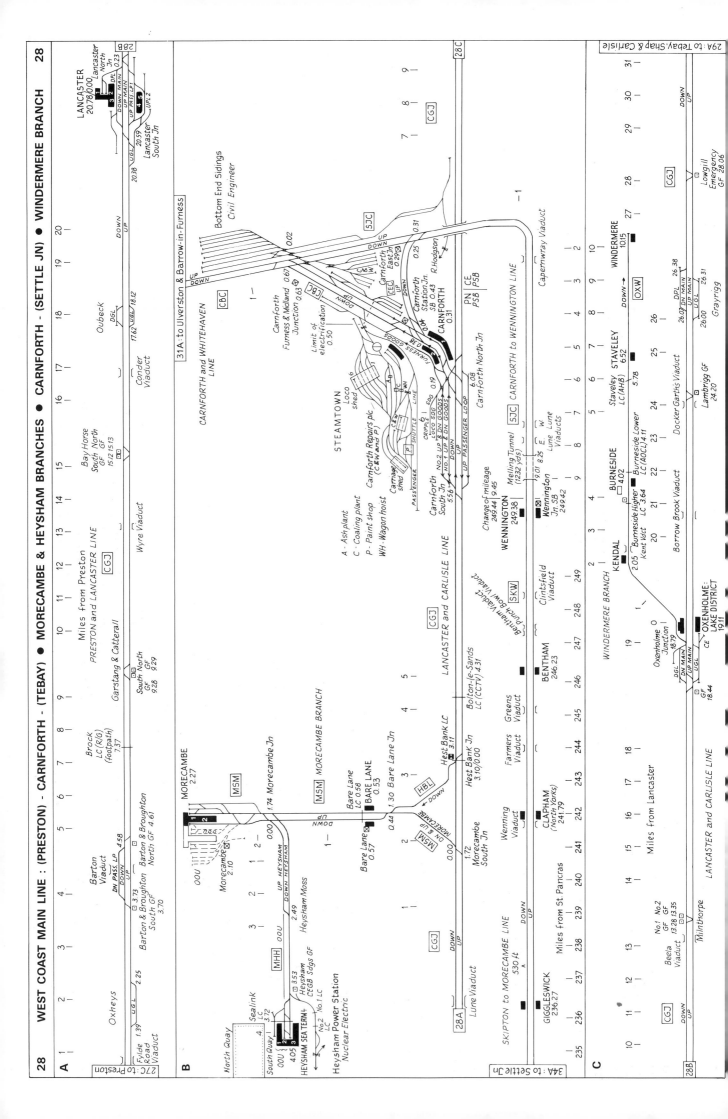

WEST COAST MAIN LINE : TEBAY - CARLISLE - KINGMOOR

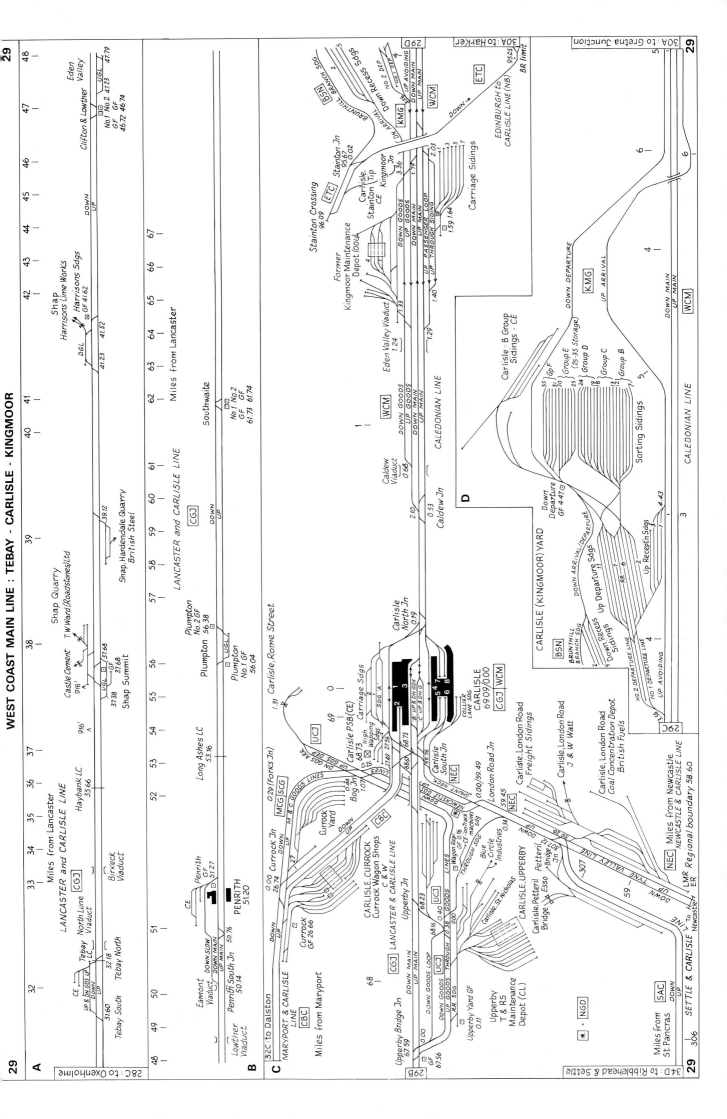

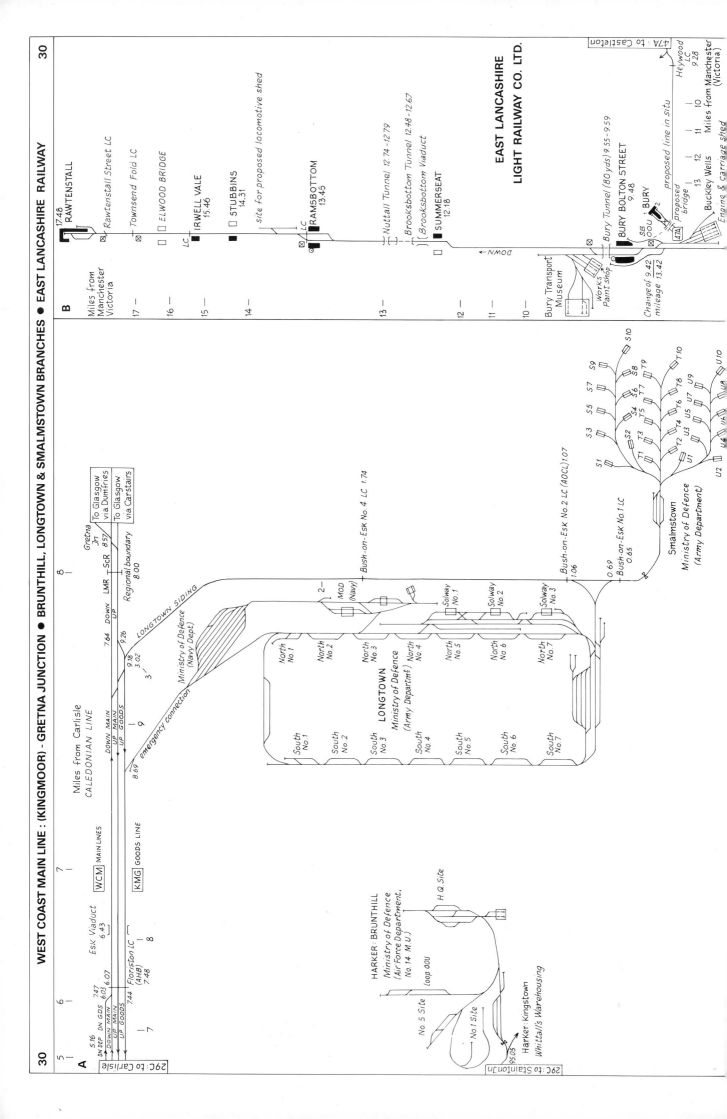

WEST COAST MAIN LINE : (KINGMOOR) - GRETNA JUNCTION ● BRUNTHILL, LONGTOWN & SMALMSTOWN BRANCHES ● EAST LANCASHIRE RAILWAY

EAST LANCASHIRE LIGHT RAILWAY CO. LTD.

RAWTENSTALL 17.48

Rawtenstall Street LC

Townsend Fold LC

☐ ELWOOD BRIDGE

LC

IRWELL VALE 15.46

☒ ☐ STUBBINS 14.31

site for proposed locomotive shed

LC

RAMSBOTTOM 13.45

Nuttall Tunnel 12.74-12.79

Brooksbottom Tunnel 12.48-12.67

[Brooksbottom Viaduct

SUMMERSEAT 12.18

←DOWN

Bury Transport Museum

Works Paint shop

Bury Tunnel (80 yds) 9.55-9.59

SB ; BURY
OOU 2

BURY BOLTON STREET 9.48

Change of 9.42
Bury mileage 13.42

47A

47A : to Castleton

Heywood LC 9.28

proposed line in situ

Buckley Wells

proposed bridge

Engine & carriage shed

Miles from Manchester (Victoria)

B

Miles from Manchester Victoria

17 —

16 —

15 —

14 —

13 —

12 —

11 —

10 —

WEST COAST MAIN LINE (left section)

A

Miles from Carlisle
CALEDONIAN LINE

Gretna Jn.
8 —

To Glasgow via Dumfries

To Glasgow via Carstairs

ScR 8.57

Regional boundary 8.00

LMR

7.64 DOWN UP

DOWN MAIN
UP MAIN
UP GOODS

9.26

9.18
3.02

3 —

9 —
6 —

LONGTOWN SIDING

emergency connection
8.69

Ministry of Defence (Navy Dept)

2 —
MOD (Navy)

Bush-on-Esk No. 4 LC LC 1.74

Solway No.1

Solway No.2

Solway No.3

North No.1
North No.2
North No.3
North No.4
North No.5
North No.6
North No.7

LONGTOWN
Ministry of Defence (Army Department)

South No.1
South No.2
South No.3
South No.4
South No.5
South No.6
South No.7

Bush-on-Esk No.2 LC (AOCL) 1.07
1.06

0.69

Bush-on-Esk No.1 LC
0.65

Smalmstown
Ministry of Defence (Army Department)

S10
S9
S8 T10
S7 T9
S6 T8
S5 T7 T5
S4 T6
S3 T4 U9
S2 T3 U7 U10
T2 U5
S1 T1 U3 U8
U1 U6 U4A U10
U2 U4

WCM MAIN LINES

KMG GOODS LINE

Esk Viaduct 6.43

Floriston LC
(AHB)
7.48

8 —

Miles from Carlisle

5.16 DN DEP DN GDS
747
6.03 6.07

744

DOWN MAIN
UP MAIN
UP GOODS

7 —
6 —

29C: to Carlisle

HARKER : BRUNTHILL
Ministry of Defence (Air Force Department, No.14 M.U.)

H.Q. Site

loop OOU

No.5 Site

No.1 Site

Harker : Kingstown
Whittall's Warehousing

29C: to Staintonan

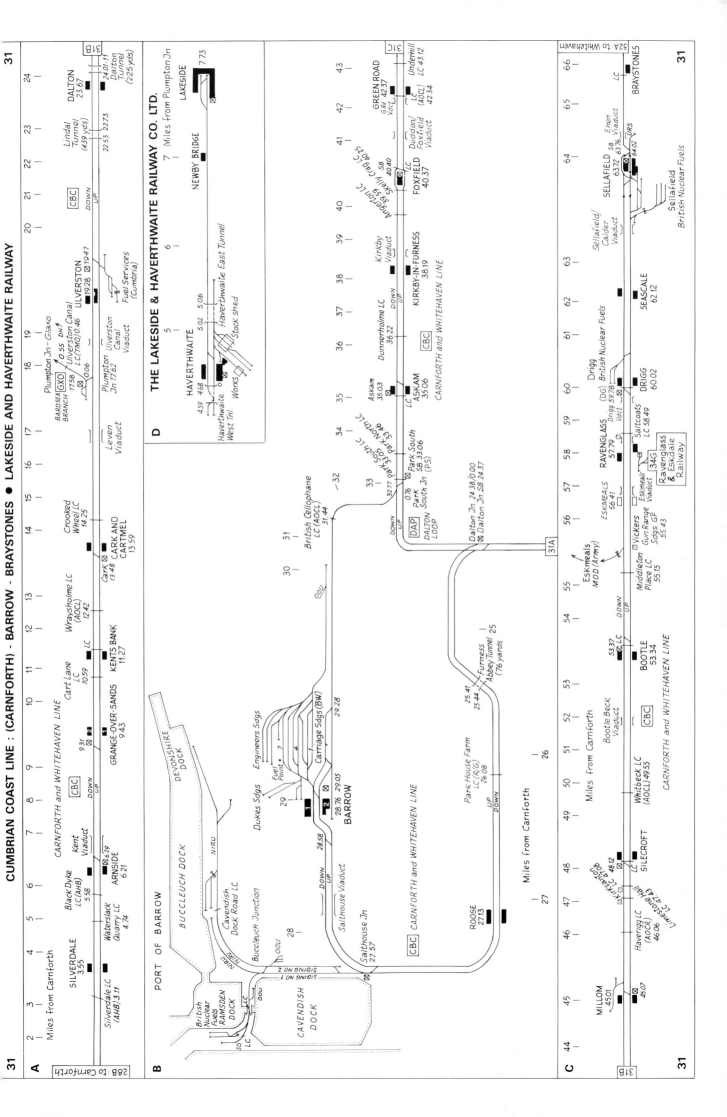

CUMBRIAN COAST LINE : (CARNFORTH) - BARROW - BRAYSTONES ● LAKESIDE AND HAVERTHWAITE RAILWAY

THE LAKESIDE & HAVERTHWAITE RAILWAY CO. LTD.

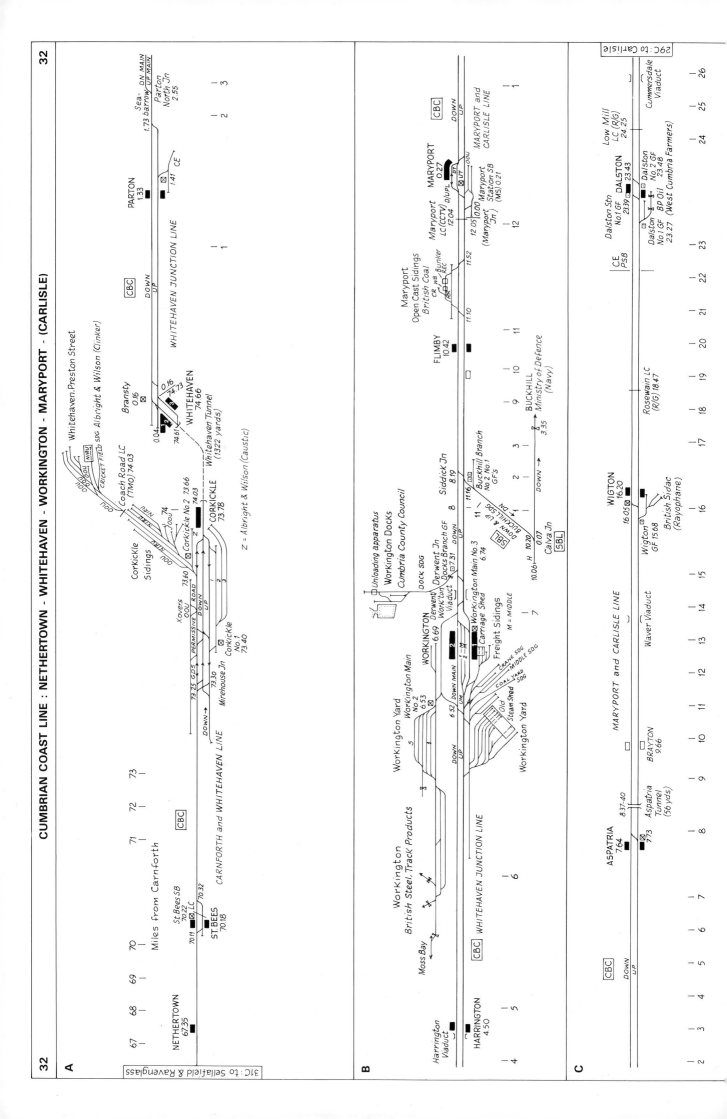

A

Miles from Carnforth

Whitehaven, Preston Street

Sea-on MAIN
1.73 barrow UP MAIN

Parton North Jn 2.55

PARTON 1.33
CE 1.41

CBC DOWN / UP
WHITEHAVEN JUNCTION LINE

CRICKET FIELD SDG Albright & Wilson (Clinker)

Bransty 0.16
0.16

0.04
74.73
2 74.61

WHITEHAVEN 74.66
Whitehaven Tunnel (1322 yards)

Coach Road LC (TMO) 74.03
NIRU

Corkickle Sidings
Corkickle No 2 73.66
74
CORKICKLE 73.78

Z = Albright & Wilson (Caustic)

73.60

Xovers
OOU
DOWN ROAD
73.25 GDS PERMISSIVE
2
3

Corkickle No 1 73.40

73.30
Mirehouse Jn

DOWN →

CARNFORTH and WHITEHAVEN LINE

St Bees SB 70.22
LC 70.32
ST BEES 70.18
70.11

NETHERTOWN 67.35

CBC

31C: to Sellafield & Ravenglass

67 68 69 70 71 72 73

B

Workington British Steel, Track Products

Moss Bay

Harrington Viaduct
HARRINGTON 4.50

CBC
WHITEHAVEN JUNCTION LINE

Unloading apparatus
Workington Docks Cumbria County Council

DOCK SDG

Derwent Jn
6.69
Work'ton Docks Branch GF
Workington Viaduct
Derwent

WORKINGTON 6.53
Workington Main No 2
Workington Yard
Carriage Shed
Workington Main No 3 6.74

DOWN MAIN
UM
2 - M
M = MIDDLE
Freight Sidings
7

CRANE SDG
COAL YARD
Old Steam Shed
MIDDLE SDG

Workington Yard

DOWN / UP
5

Calva Jn
SBL
10.06
10.20
0.07

Workton Docks Branch GF 7.31

Siddick Jn 8.19

Buckhill Branch No 2 No 1 GF's

1 2 3
DOWN →

BUCKHILL DN
11.16
DOWN & UP SDG
SBS

11

FLIMBY 10.42

Maryport Open Cast Sidings British Coal

11.10
11.52
CR WB Bunker
RR Rec

MARYPORT 0.27
D/UPL UT
Maryport LC (CCTV) 12.04
12.05 Maryport Station SB
1000 Maryport Jn (Maryport Jn) (MS) 0.21

CBC DOWN / UP
MARYPORT and CARLISLE LINE

4 5 6 7 8 9 10 11 12 13 14 15 16 17 18 19 20 21 22 23 24 25 26

BUCKHILL Ministry of Defence (Navy)
3.35

C

ASPATRIA 7.64
7.73
Aspatria Tunnel (56 yds)
8.37-40

BRAYTON 9.66

Waver Viaduct

WIGTON 16.20
16.05
Wigton GF 15.68
British Sidac (Rayophane)

Rosewain LC (R/G) 18.47

CE
PSB

Dalston Stn
DALSTON 23.39 No 1 GF
Dalston No 2 GF 23.48
Dalston No 1 GF 23.27 (West Cumbria Farmers)
BP Oil
23.43

Low Mill LC (R/G) 24.25

Cummersdale Viaduct

29C: to Carlisle

CBC DOWN / UP
MARYPORT and CARLISLE LINE

2 3 4 5 6 7 8 9 10 11 12 13 14 15 16 17 18 19 20 21 22 23 24 25 26

A

33B

FHR

Blackburn Tunnel (435 yards)

10.75
10.55

BLACKBURN 10.42

Blackburn Tunnel

13 1   2   4

UP & DN THROUGH
UP & DOWN
DN THRO'
UP
MAIN

Blackburn, King Street British Fuels

Blackburn Bolton Jn

Taylor Street SDG 9.60

Blackburn Bolton Rd.

MILL HILL (Lancs) 9.24

Goods shed 23.60

Blackburn, P & G Fogarty

Blackburn Branch Jn

Blackburn Bolton Branch Jn

Blackburn Freight Sdgs (East Lancs Sidings)

BBR

48A: to Darwen and Bolton

BOLTON to BLACKBURN LINE

UP & DOWN DARWEN DOWN

24.08
24
10.11

CHERRY TREE 8.50

Pleasington Viaduct 7.73

PLEASINGTON 7.43

Houghton Tower Viaduct 6.54

Miles from Farington Curve Junction

Houghton LC (AHB) 5.27

Houghton GF's 5.32

Hospital LC
Gregson Lane LC & GF 3.71
Bamford LC
O'rams No.1 LC
O'rams No.2
Bannister LC

Bamber Bridge Stn. LC GF 2.32

Bamber Bridge Station
Bamber Bridge CE

CE's Sdgs GF 2.10

BAMBER BRIDGE 2.29

Bamber Bridge W.H. Bowker

Whittle International GF 1.70

PRESTON to BLACKBURN LINE

27C: to Preston

DOWN UP

FHR

Controlled from Preston (PN) PSB

B

33C

FHR

To Hebden Bridge

Regional boundary 22.62

ER LMR

DN J
UP Y

Eastwood GF 22.34

Cockden Viaduct

Horsfall Tunnel (274 yds) 20.44-56

Castle Hill Tunnel (194 yds) 20.07-20.16

Millwood Tnl (225y) 20.07-20.16

Miles from Manchester (Vic)

MVN

Y = Whitley Viaduct
Z = Lobb Mill Viaduct

Hall Royd Jn 30.54 19.61

MANCHESTER and NORMANTON LINE

19.49 to Todmorden & Rochdale

47B: to Todmorden & Rochdale

Stansfield Hall

30.49
30.24
30.17

DJH

DOWN UP

GISBURN Tunnel (157 yds) 28.57-64

Stockbeck Viaduct 29.07

COLNE 27.41

Chaffers Sdg LC Colne Vdct 25.62

GJC

NELSON 25.35

Nelson Vdct

BRIERFIELD 24.20

Brierfield Tnl (73 yds) 24.37-40

Swan Side Viaduct 24.65

Chatburn 23.23

BURNLEY BARRACKS

Gannow Jn 21.38

Burnley Vdct

BURNLEY CENTRAL 22.05

BURNLEY MANCHESTER RD. 21.67

Towneley LC 22.46

Towneley Tunnel (398 yards)

FHR BURNLEY BRANCH

749ft Copy Pit
25.52-65 26.20

Holme Tunnel (265 yards)

Portsmouth LC (R/G) 27.30

Kitson Wood Tunnel (290 yards)

Lydgate Viaduct 28.69
28.76 29.10

BLACKBURN to HELLIFIELD LINE (NORTH LANCASHIRE LINE)

Horrocksford Castle Cement

Horrocksford Jn

21.46 21.60

CLITHEROE (occasional use) 20.77

Low Moor LC (CCTV) 20.77

Primrose Viaduct

Padiham Power Stn.

National Power

PRG

1.76
1.58
1.56

NORTH LANCASHIRE LOOP

ROSE GROVE 20.32

Rose Grove West Jn 20.05

DOWN GOODS
DN MAIN
UP MAIN
UP GOODS

0.00

HAPTON 18.73

HUNCOAT 17.41

Huncoat Stn. LC GF 17.36

Whalley 17.61

Whalley Viaduct No.41

ACCRINGTON 15.64

Accrington Vdct 15.78

Accrington GF 15.56

Langho 15.54

Wilpshire Tunnel (327 yds)

CHURCH & OSWALDTWISTLE 14.76

Church Viaduct 14.65

15.14 15.41

DGL
DM
UP MAIN

RISHTON 13.26

Rishton Tunnel (68 yds)

Wilpshire 13.38 13.71 14.06
OOU

Shore Farm LC 13.26 13.71

Daisyfield Jn 11.25

Daisyfield LC 11.09

Cobwall Viaduct 11.64 11.48

11.30

PN PSB

DOWN UP

BLACKBURN to COLNE LINE

FHR

33A

Miles from Farington Curve Jn

Controlled from Preston (PN) PSB

C

34A: to Settle

SKW

23.50
23.14

DRS

UP MN
UP GOODS LOOP

DOWN MAIN

HELLIFIELD SB 231.21
Hellifield 231.14

Haw Lane LC 230.68

33B

DJH

DOWN UP

BLACKBURN to HELLIFIELD LINE

RYLSTONE Tilcon (P.W. Spencer Lime)

7.09

6.50 BR Limit

GARGRAVE 224.79

Rylstone LC (TMO) 5.17

GRASSINGTON or SWINDEN BRANCH

DOWN →

SKS

SKIPTON to MORECAMBE LINE

222.08

(Skipton North Jn) 221.68

TJC SKW 221.62

Skipton Station North Jn 221.21

Skipton Station 222.68 222.30

DOWN THROUGH
UP MAIN
UP GOODS LOOP
DN THRO'
DN TDG

3 4   2

Skipton North SB 221.33

Skipton Stn South SB 221.13

Skipton Stn South Jn 221.21

SKS TJC

Haw Bank Tunnel (220 yds) 220.64 10.00 (Embsay Jn)

34F: Yorkshire Dales Railway

221.07 220.77

LEEDS and BRADFORD EXTENSION LINE

DOWN UP

Snaygill Regional boundary 219.05

ER LMR

To Keighley

Miles from St Pancras

219 — 220

221 222 223 224 225 226 227 228 229 230 231

34   33

33

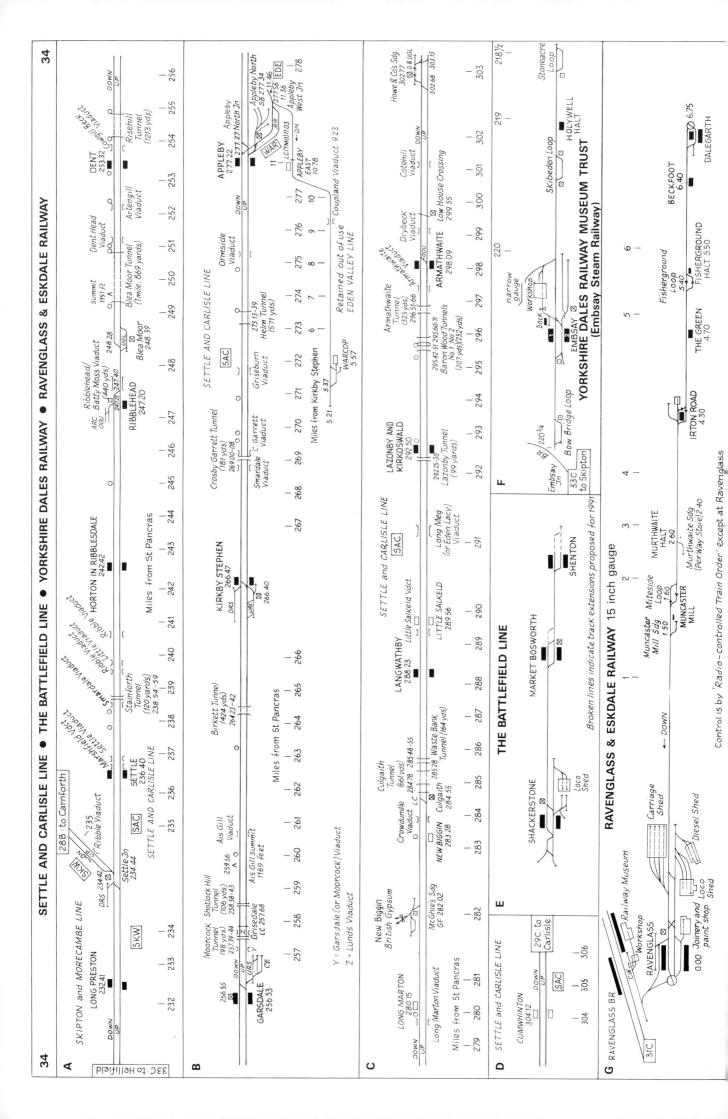

SETTLE AND CARLISLE LINE ● THE BATTLEFIELD LINE ● YORKSHIRE DALES RAILWAY ● RAVENGLASS & ESKDALE RAILWAY

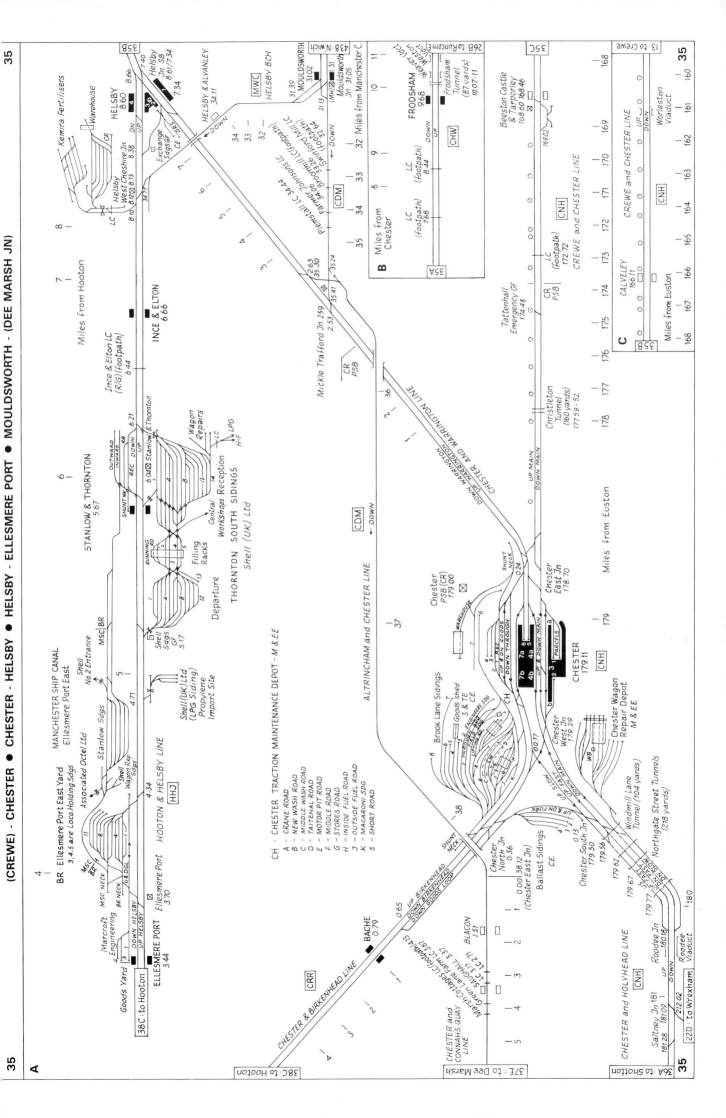

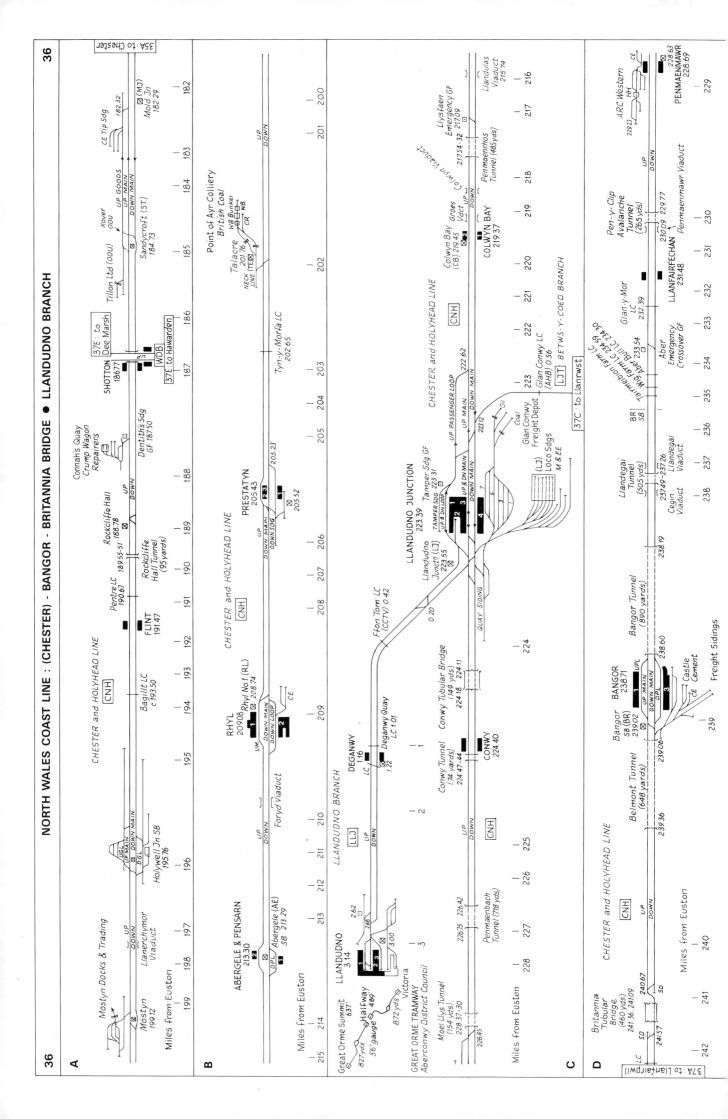

A

AMLWCH
Associated Octel

Rhosgoch
Anglesey
Borough Council
15.51

LLANERCH-Y-MEDD
11.06

Cleifiog Uchaf LC (VV) 260.07

Clefiog Uchaf LC 260.57

BR limit 17.37

Gantry

Freight Sidings

VALLEY 260.09

Stanley Embankment

RHOSGOCH 14.06

RHOSNEIGR 256.04

Trewin Sands Viaduct

TY CROES 254.31
LC 254.32
Xover OOU

LLANGWYLLOG 7.10

LLANGEFNI 4.41

Llangefni LC 3.74

BODORGAN 251.52

Bodorgan No.1 Tunnel (413 yds) 250.78-59

Bodorgan No.2 Tunnel (115 yards)

Bodorgan Viaduct 249.74-65

Gaerwen SB
Freight Sdgs 0.13
Gaerwen Jn 0.00
245.15

Llanddaniel LC (R/g) 243.75

LLANFAIRPWLL 242.29

LC 245.09

BR SB 242.22

36D: to Bangor

37D

ANGLESEY CENTRAL LINE

GLA

CHESTER and HOLYHEAD LINE

CNH

Miles from Euston

B

Holyhead Container Terminal
Sealink UK
Container Terminal
LHS

Holyhead Freight Terminal SB
263.47

* Holyhead SB (HD) 263.26

Holyhead Loco Inspection Point (HD)
M & EE

Anglesey Aluminium Metals Ltd (Rio Tinto)

Holyhead Cattle Dock
Stockton Haulage

Crane Roads 1-4

HOLYHEAD
263.52
263.49
263.57

Stn GF

Carriage Shed No.1
Carriage Shed No.2
Stockton Haulage

Holyhead Old Yard

INNER HARBOUR

NIRU
261.56
263.07

Miles from Euston
261 262 263

CNH

37A

36C: to Llandudno Jn

37B

C

GLAN CONWY 1.39

Miles from Llandudno Junction

CONWY VALLEY LINE

LJT

DOWN

D

Miles from Llandudno Junction

PONT-Y-PANT 19.29

Pont-y-Pant Upper Tunnel (66 yds) 19.56-59

Pont-y-Pant Lower Tunnel (144 yds) 19.10-17

DOLWYDDELAN 20.62

ROMAN BRIDGE 22.48

Roman Bridge Tunnel (43 yds) 22.55-57

Bertheos Tunnel (46 yds) 22.19-22

TAL-Y-CAFN 5.05
LC

DOLGARROG 8.12
LC

Tyn-Ddol LC 9.73

Tan Lan LC 10.31 11.08

LLANRWST 11.17
LC 11.22

LLANRWST NORTH 11.57

Llanrwst 11.08

Llanrwst Tunnel (85 yards) 11.50-11.54

BETWS-Y-COED 15.02

Beaverpool Tunnel (110 yds) 16.10-19

Gethin's Bridge

BETWS-Y-COED BRANCH · BETWS-Y-COED & FESTINIOG LINE

37D

Miles from Bala Junction
19 20 21

LJT

Ffestiniog Tunnel (2 miles, 333 yds) 24.33x 790 ft

GF No.1 27.07
GF No.2 27.33
GF No.3 27.51
GF No.4

BLAENAU FFESTINIOG 27.40
CoM 27.53/25.25 (LMS/GW)
SDG
Ffestiniog Rly

Cwmbowydd LC (TMO) 25.15

Fronlas LC 24.07

Bryn-yr-Odyn Viaduct 21.15

Gelly Viaduct (108 yds) 25.02

TRAWSFYNYDD
GF OOU 20.6

MAENTWROG ROAD 20.02
(special trains only)

18.76
18.54
Nuclear Electric

BLAENAU FESTINIOG BRANCH

Miles from Bidston

To Portmadoc 24.7

E

Croes Newydd North Fork SB 0.68

Wrexham Exchange Jn

Miles from Wrexham Central

GWERSYLLT 2.29

CEFN-Y-BEDD 4.20

Cefn-y-Bedd Viaduct 4.11

CAERGWRLE 4.73

HOPE 5.44

PENYFFORD 7.39
7.41

HOPE EXCHANGE 7.64

Penyffford Castle Cement 8.08

BUCKLEY 8.69

HAWARDEN 10.64

Miles from Wrexham Central

WDB

WREXHAM, MOLD AND CONNAH'S QUAY LINE

To Wrexham 22D

HAWARDEN BRIDGE 14.12

SHOTTON 13.00

River Dee TOWER SDG

Dee Marsh Jn SB 13.78

13.33 14.15

13.40/6.10

36A: to Flint

36A: to Chester

CNH

NG

Change of mileage

DEE MARSH
Shotton Works
British Steel

CE & M & EE

To Weighbridge

Dee Marsh Jn

Birkenhead Sidings

Dee Marsh North Jn

NORTH WALES and LIVERPOOL LINE

Dee Marsh Deeside Titanium

WDB

NMDQ

DOWN

Shotwick OOU GF 11.76

Shotwick Occupation LC 12.25

Shotwick GF 5.50

Shotwick Paper Co. Ltd

BURTON POINT 10.64

LC (footpath) 5.61

CCG
CDM

39A: to Bidston

Miles from Chester East Jn

Miles from Chester

35A: to Mickle Trafford Jn and Helsby

CHESTER and CONNAH'S QUAY LINE

HALTON JUNCTION - RUNCORN - (SPEKE JUNCTION) ● DITTON - (WARRINGTON) ● (CHESTER/ELLESMERE PORT - ROCK FERRY

A

T Plasmor

Widnes, Tanhouse Lane, Blue Circle Cement

Widnes, Carterhouse Jn
ICI Pilkington
Tan House La LC
RECEIVER
Sullivan Wks
LC
Sullivan Sdg GF 16.00
15 18 38B
16

Widnes, Carterhouse Jn Tarmac
Widnes, Carterhouse Jn. 16.28
UP GOODS
OOU
DOWN GOODS
17 Miles from Skelton Jn

Z Creosoting Shed

DITTON CREOSOTING DEPOT
Civil Engineer

RECEPTION ROAD
EMERGENCY ROAD
TIMBER RD 2
Z
CHAIR RD
CHAIR RD 2
MACHINE RD
DEAL SHED
SAWMILL
LINES 1,2,&2
PROP YARD
POLE ROAD
OXO 2
OXO 1
OOU

WIDNES SOUTH 17.18

Widnes Yard
Widnes Marcham
Ditton Viaduct

Runcorn Bridge (River Mersey) (915 yds)

UP MAIN
DOWN MAIN
UP GOODS
DOWN GOODS
SDJ
British Oxygen Co

182 —
181 —
180 —

DITTON 182.79
Ditton Jn No.2 (DN2)
182.62
182.62
Ditton Jn No.1 (DN1) 182.71
18.55
163.02
4.5
UP GOODS
DOWN GOODS
183.12

RUNCORN 180.40
NIRU
(RN) 180.33 180.30
Runcorn Jn
003
THRO SDG 0.30
RUNCORN DOCK BRANCH SD
BR limit 0.72
Folly Lane GF 0.63
0.47
RDB
FOLLY LANE

Castner Kellner Wks. ICI
Rock Savage Works – ICI
BR Sdgs
Docks
Weston Salt Works ICI

Halton Jn (HN) 179.20
0.00 179.24
DN
26B : to Frodsham/Acton Bridge

WJL   RUNCORN BRANCH

184   Miles from Euston

B

TIMPERLEY and GARSTON LINE
WJL

UP FAST
DOWN FAST
UP SLOW
DOWN SLOW
UP/DN R
184.54
185.to
Halewood Ford Motor Co

Garston Silcock Express
Speke Jn. GF 186.72
Ramps
186
187

FIDDLERS FERRY POWER STATION
PowerGen
Control Building
Coal Track Hoppers
HOPPER APPROACH TRACKS
LC (open) WB
LC (open)
FLASH SDG
LC (open) WB
CR SDG
DEP RD NO 1
DEP RD NO 2
ARRIVAL
M B E E
Fiddlers Ferry SB
14.46
Marsh House LC (CCTV) 14.10

Johnstones Lane LC (footpath) 15.41
UP GOODS
DOWN GOODS
Sullivan Sdg GF 16.00
SDJ

TIMPERLEY and GARSTON LINE
Fiddlers Ferry LC 13.83 LC 13.63
Penketh Hall LC 13.31
Sankey Bridges LC (footpath) 12.83
Monks Sdg LC 11.70
Litton's Mill Crossing 11.45
26B : to Arpley Jn

13 14 15 16   Miles from Skelton Jn

40 : to Garston & Liverpool Lime Street
38A

C

Ellesmere Port Docks
Cawoods (1 mile)

MANCHESTER SHIP CANAL
Ellesmere Port West
(approx distances from Ellesmere Port, BR)

Jakes Rail Tank Cleaning
35A : to Helsby
ELLESMERE PORT 3.44
3.37
3.44

Manisty Wharf 1¾ miles
Gulf Oil (1½ miles)
LS
Dock Rd LC
Richard Lawson Transport
West End Sdgs
WBL
WST

OVERPOOL 2.28

Panocean Storage & Transport Eastham 3½ miles
Unitank Storage Co Ltd 3½ miles

LITTLE SUTTON 1.47

35A : to Chester

CR PSB

CAPENHURST 5.11

HHJ
DOWN HELSBY
UP HELSBY
HOOTON & HELSBY LINE
DOWN BIRKENHEAD
UP BIRKENHEAD
CHESTER & BIRKENHEAD LINE
CRR

HOOTON 8.08
Hooton South Jn 0.02
BAY
SIDING RR
8.08
7.68
Hooton SB 7.73
Hooton North Jn (Merseyside PTE boundary)
8.17

BROMBOROUGH
Van den Burgh & Jurgens
CRR

Tunnel LC (open)
Lorry Park LC (AOCL)
Commercial Road LC (TMO)
Magazine Lane LC (AOCL)
RIVERSIDE SDG RR
FACTORY SDG
RR SDG

BROMBOROUGH RAKE 10.38
BROMBOROUGH 9.71

Lubrizol RR
Rainbow Bridge
Pt. Sunlight Loop
PLATFORM RR
Pt. SUNLIGHT SDG
11.42

SPITAL 11.16
PORT SUNLIGHT 11.61
BEBINGTON 12.36

Rock Ferry South Jn 13.30

DOWN MAIN
UP MAIN

CHESTER and BIRKENHEAD LINE

9 10 11 12 13   Miles from Chester
4 5 6 7 8   Miles from Chester

39A : to Birkenhead

WIRRAL : ROCK FERRY - BIRKENHEAD - NEW BRIGHTON/WEST KIRBY ● BIDSTON - NESTON

A

BIRKENHEAD PARK [BEN] and NEW BRIGHTON LINE

New Brighton 7.06
WALL SDG
SDG 2
NEW BRIGHTON 7.18
☒

7 —
1 —

WALLASEY GROVE ROAD 5.73

WALLASEY VILLAGE 5.48

6 —

BIDSTON ORE DOCK
Mersey Docks & Harbour Co.

5 —

National Fuel Distributors
Limit of electrification

BIRKENHEAD PARK [BEN] and NEW BRIGHTON LINE

(Seacombe Jn) 4.62

DOWN SDG
UP SDG

Bidston West Jn 4.71
[CWK]

Bidston Dee Jn 4.77
BIDSTON 4.75

School Lane LC 4.71
1.009
Merseyside PTE boundary

Bidston East Jn 4.40
☒
Birkenhead North No 2 SB 4.22

[WDB]

NORTH WALES and LIVERPOOL LINE

Storeton LC (footpath) 4.31

crossover OOU

UPTON 1.67

HESWALL 6.03

NESTON 8.55

[39B]
37E : to Hawarden Bridge

1 —
2 —
3 —
4 —
5 —
6 —
7 —
8 —
9 —
10—

DOWN
UP

5 —
6 —

Spillers

EAST FLOAT

Warehouse
Lifting Bridge
WEST FLOAT

Vittoria Dock
Stanton Grove Warehos.

Duke Street LC

NIRU
OOU

MERSEY DOCKS & HARBOUR CO'S LINES

BR | MDHC
0.43
Wallasey Bridge Rd.LC 0.36

COAL SDG
UP GOODS
DN GDS
UP GDS

BIRKENHEAD NORTH TMD (emu) (BD)
M&EE
Birkenhead North No.1 3.78

Birkenhead North ☒ 3
BIRKENHEAD NORTH 3.75

[CWK]

Cavendish St Tunnel (71 yards)
3.19 3.15
BIRKENHEAD PARK 3.05

3.48 3.45
Corporation Road Tunnel (64 yards)

BIRKENHEAD PARK and NEW BRIGHTON LINE

1 —
4 —
3 —

Canning St.North 15.29
LC 15.26

Cathcart Street LC (closed)
MDHC BR 15.40

MDHC LINES

MERSEY RAILWAY
Mersey Tunnel (Park Branch)
2.69

[CWK]

Canning St North

40 : to Liverpool
Mann Island
Mersey Tunnel 069
[MIR]
Canning Street Jn 1.60

HAMILTON SQUARE 1.67 (plat/m 3.168)
Hamilton Square Jn 1.72
1 2 3

JS PSB
1.4.81

Inspection Depot M&EE

[CC5] GREEN LANE to CATHCART ST. LINE (Chester & Birkenhead)

UP WIRRAL
DOWN WIRRAL

Haymarket Tunnel (139 yds) 2.24
Lorne Street LC 1.4.64
BAY

BIRKENHEAD CENTRAL 2.30
Birkenhead Central 2.34

DOWN GOODS
UP GOODS

Hinderton Field Tunnel (497 yards) 2.64
GREEN LANE 2.64
Green Lane Tunnel (59 yards) 2.66
2.39

14 —
3 —

Rock Ferry North Jn

Rock Ferry 13.60
Rock Ferry 3.35
UP 8 UP GDS

ROCK FERRY 3.42/13.43

Rock Ferry 3.46/13.39
Rock Ferry South Jn 13.30

[MIR]
[CRR]

38C : to Hooton

1 —
2 —
3 —

MERSEY RAILWAY

UP MERSEY 2.61
DOWN MERSEY 3.23

B

WEST KIRBY to SEACOMBE LINE (Wirral)

[CWK]

W Kirby 10.36
WEST KIRBY
Station Rd.LC 10.46
LC 9.60
Drummond Rd (Footpath)

HOYLAKE 9.27
9.32 ☒
Elm Grove LC 9.31

MANOR ROAD 8.71
Meadowcroft LC 9.00

MEOLS 8.11
Bertram Drive LC 8.58

Carr Lane LC 7.53
Prospect Farm LC 7.35

TOWN MEADOW (site for new stn) 7.19
Leighton Ave LC (footpath) 7.8.28

Cartron Lane Avenue LC 7.19

Moreton 6.23

MORETON 6.29

Reeds Lane LC 5.61
☒ SB 5.61
LEASOWE 5.65

Melrose Avenue LC 9.05
Sandringham Avenue LC 8.65

1 —
2 —
3 —
4 —
5 —
6 —
7 —
8 —
9 —
10—

DOWN
UP

[39A]

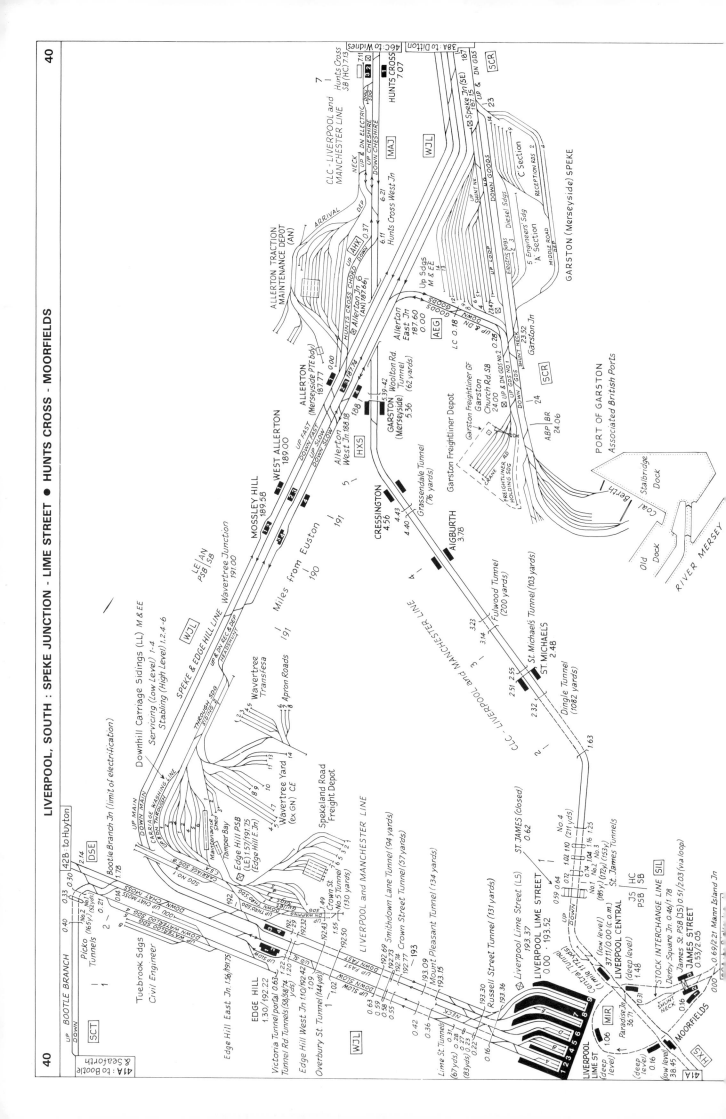

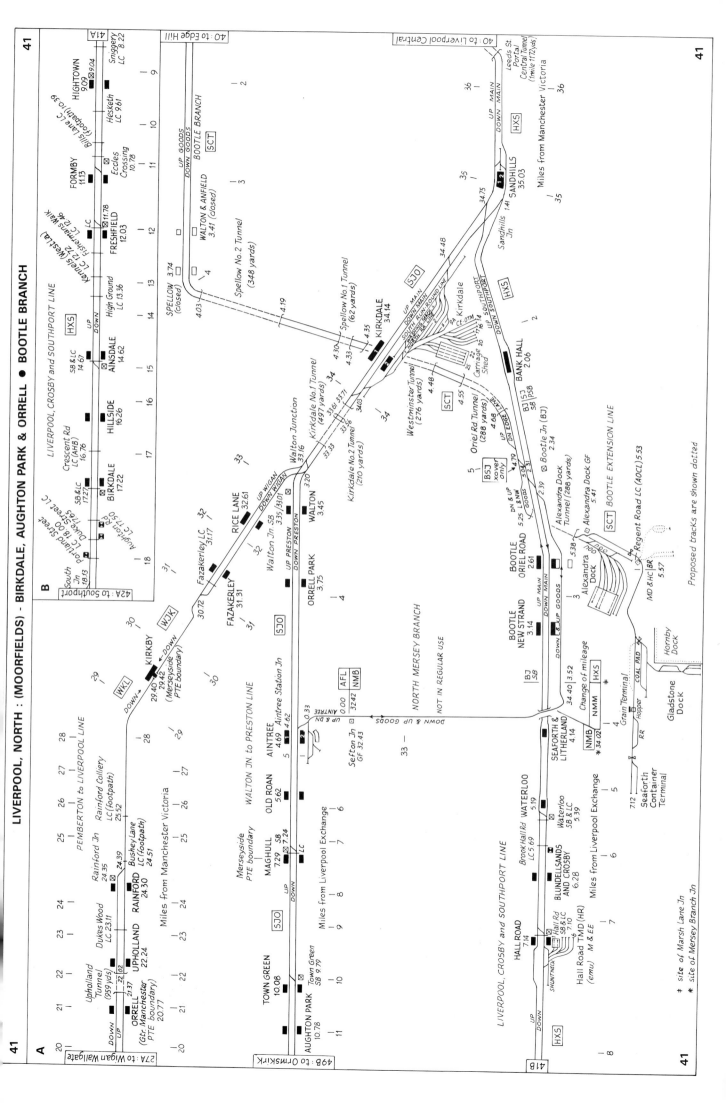

LIVERPOOL, NORTH : (MOORFIELDS) - BIRKDALE, AUGHTON PARK & ORRELL ● BOOTLE BRANCH

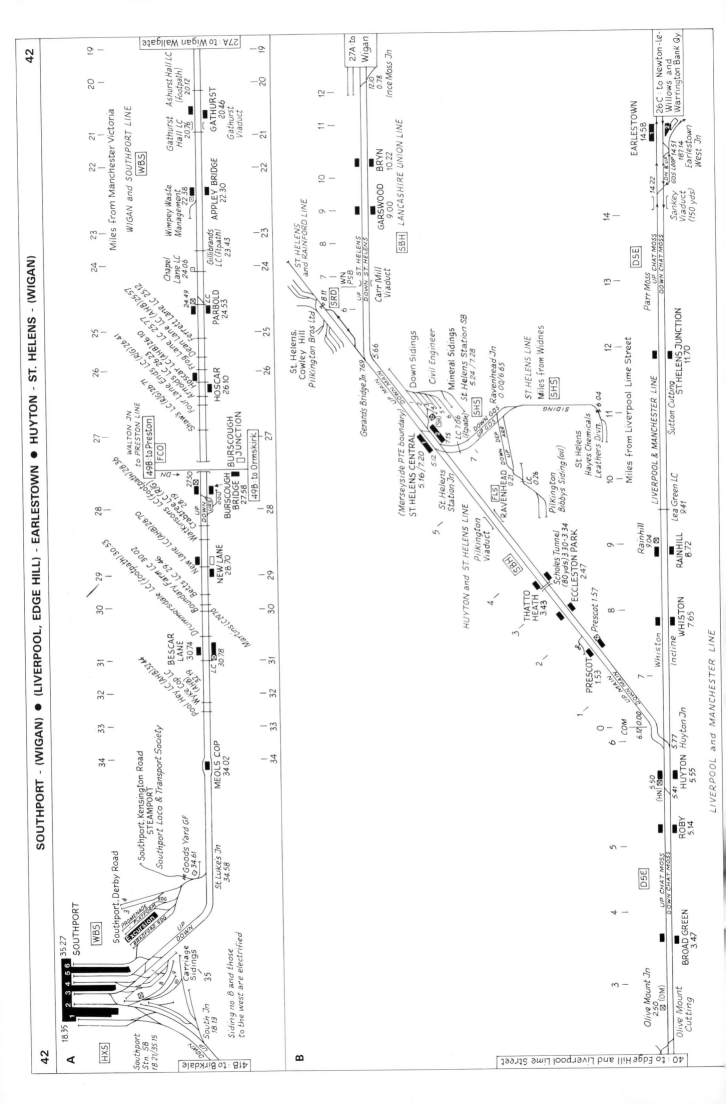

43

ETRURIA - CHEADLE HULME ● (CREWE) - CHEADLE HULME ● MOULDSWORTH ● KNUTSFORD ● SANDBACH - NORTHWICH ● WILMSLOW - HEALD GREEN

43

A

25B: to Stoke-on-Trent

MACCLESFIELD and COLWICH LINE

Shelton
British Steel
Granville Sdgs

ETRURIA 18.64

Grange Jn. SB (GE) 18.26
18.30

Miles from Macclesfield Hibel Road
18

CMD

UP GOODS
UP MAIN
DOWN MAIN
DOWN GOODS

ORE FULLS
ORE EMPTIES

Grading Sdgs C & W
Pinnox Branch Sdgs
FREIGHT DEPOT
Up Sdgs
Down Sdgs

LONGPORT 17.03
CE
Longport Jn 16.71
SB (LT)

Chatterley Sdgs

Bradwell Sdgs SB (BS) 16.29
16.24
Carless Solvents
Esso

Chatterley Valley Disposal Point
British Coal
Bunker 16 (old)
16.16
16.00 | 15.65
16 (new)

UP MAIN
DOWN MAIN
UP GOODS
DOWN GOODS

Harecastle Tunnel (260 yds)

Kidsgrove Central SB (KC) 13.66
14.13-25
14
15

CE PSB
Coopers LC 1.30
KCS
CREWE BRANCH

13.60 0.07
KIDSGROVE
13
12

Mow Cop (MC) 11.30
MD | MC SB | SB
CMD
LC (CCTV)

ALSAGER 2.33

Radway Green 4.00
Ordnance Factory

43B
13: to Crewe

B

ALTRINCHAM and CHESTER LINE (CLC)

46A: to Altrincham

KNUTSFORD 14.40
Knutsford East SB 14.36
CDM

Mobberley/S LC 18.26/18.44
Winstanley's LC 18.28

PLUMLEY 17.17
Plumley West 18.07

LOSTOCK GRALAM 19.15
GK | PY SB | SB GF 18.43

ICI Lostock East
ICI Lostock Works
Down Group Sdgs 20
ICI Wade Works

Northwich East Jn 19.77 UGL
LC 20.07

Northwich 20.49
Beech St SB
Northwich Jn 8.37

Northwich West Jn 20.74
SNJ

Worths LC 6.57
Barton's LC 5.66
Flitton's LC

CMP
Crewe & Stockport Line

Northwich, Oakleigh Sidings
Northwich, Winnington Sidings
ICI Winnington

WEST COAST MAIN LINE
26A: to Warrington

BRAKE SDG
DEPARTURE / ARRIVAL
HNO

WINNINGTON BRANCH

Hartford North Jn 22.10
GREENBANK 22.28
Hartford West Jn 22.12
Hartford East Jn

Hartford CLC Jn 23.11
HJ | GK Y SB | SB
HCN

CUDDINGTON 25.15
LC (footpath) 25.49

DELAMERE 28.11
GK SB
CDM

Mouldsworth GF 30.59
Miles from Manchester Central
35A: to Mouldsworth

British Salt
MIDDLEWICH
Brooks La LC 3.28
Middlewich LC 1.40
Higher Delacre

NORTHWICH BCH
SNJ

CGJ 26A: to Crewe

HOLMES CHAPEL 166.37
North Road Viaduct
North Rode GF 4.67

GOOSTREY 168.35
Dare Viaduct
Peover Viaduct 170.19

CHELFORD 172.17
Chelford Loop DPL
SH | WW PSB | PSB
Ainsworth LC 171.18

SANDBACH 162.50
Sandbach North Jn
Sandbach (SH) PSB 162.61
Sandbach South Jn 162.28
GK SB

Elworth Hays Chemicals
Elton Wheelock Viaduct

CONGLETON 8.12
Congleton Viaduct 7.57
CMP
43A
13: to Crewe

MACCLESFIELD and COLWICH LINE

STYAL LINE

46A: to Gatley
44A: to Stockport

HEALD GREEN 3.37
Proposed Manchester Airport Line
CDM 16.45

STYAL 17.9
Dean Viaduct
Y = Wilmslow Old Viaduct
Z = Handforth Viaduct
STY

Brook Farm LC 17.9.17
HANDFORTH 178.24
Handforth Viaduct
Wilmslow Viaduct

Cheadle Hulme (CH) SB 180.59/.000
CHEADLE HULME 180.63
WW | CH PSB | SB 180.40
180.51

BRAMHALL 1.49
(Greater Manchester PTE boundary)
Bramhall Loop

POYNTON 2.79
MD | CH SB | SB

WILMSLOW 176.71
Wilmslow (WW) PSB 176.53
Wilmslow Jn
DGL

Hope Green LC 3.70

ADLINGTON 5.15
Sunny Bank LC 5.64

Prestbury Tunnel (343 yds)
PRESTBURY 7.10
MD | CH SB | SB
Prestbury GF 7.46

ALDERLEY EDGE 175.21
Alderley Edge
South Jn North Jn
Carriage Sdgs (not elec.)
DRS 175.12/175.33

MACCLESFIELD 172.54
Roadside LC 172.54
(MD) 0.20
(Hibel Rd) 0.00 9.37
Hibel Rd Tnl (343 yds)
CMD
MCH

MACCLESFIELD BRANCH

MACCLESFIELD and COLWICH LINE

ALTRINCHAM and CHESTER LINE (CLC)

WEST GOODS LINE HWG
EAST GOODS LINE HEG
NNJ

43
43

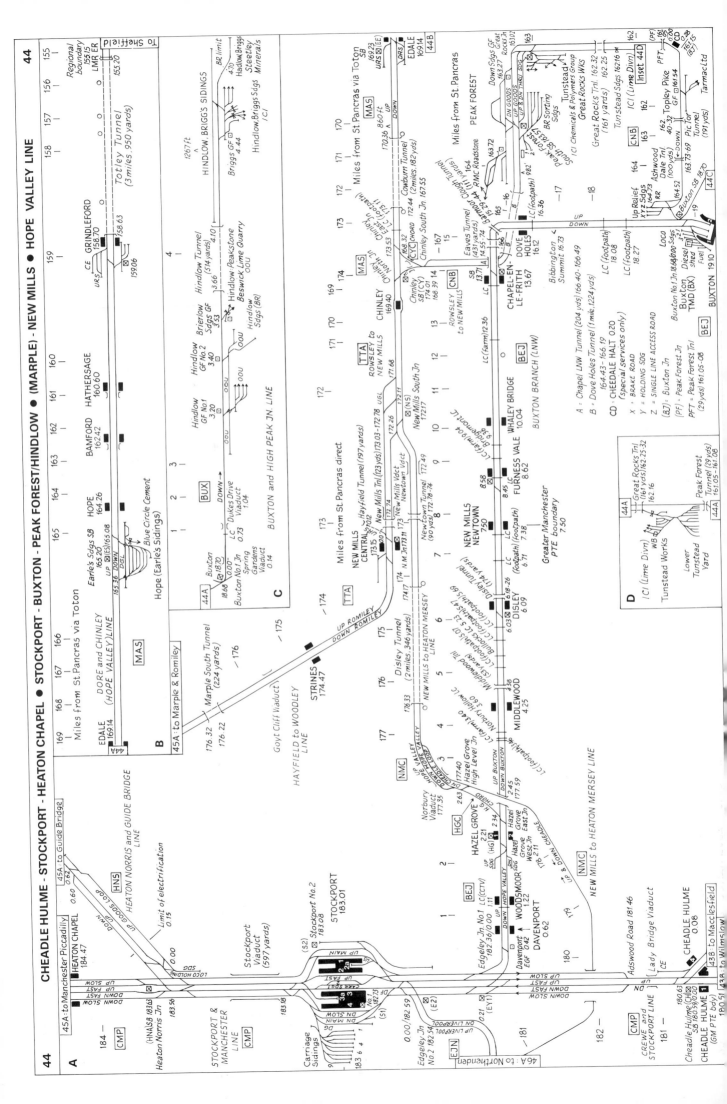

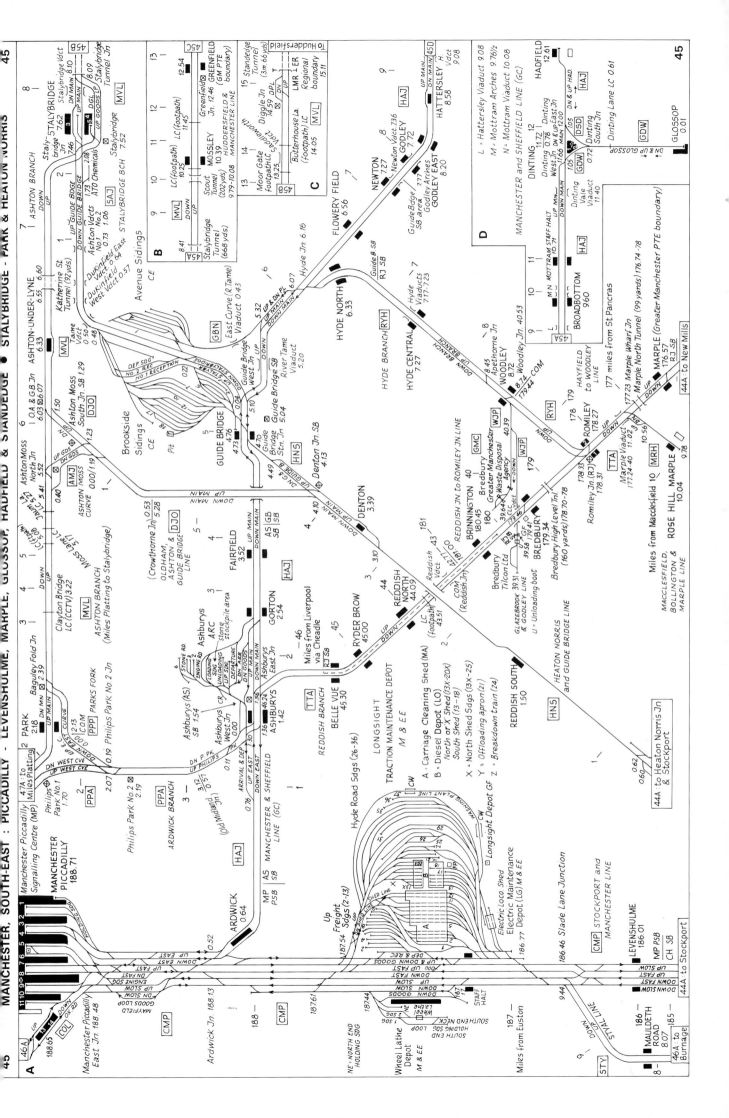

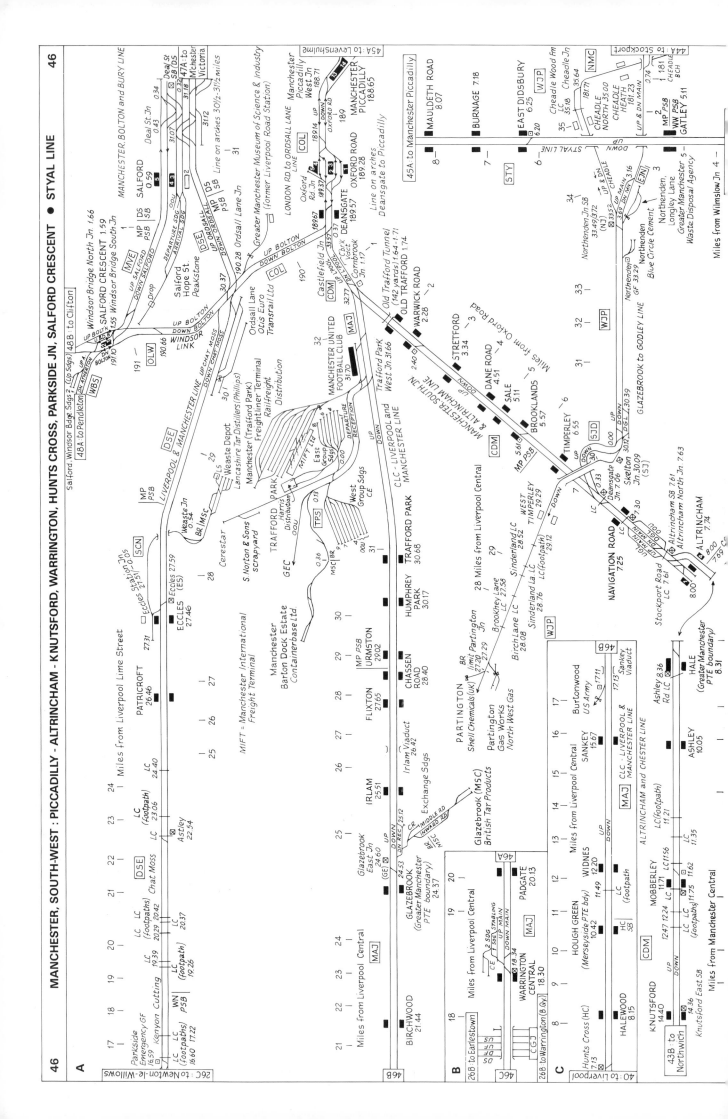

MANCHESTER, NORTH-EAST : VICTORIA – BURY, OLDHAM, ROCHDALE & TODMORDEN

Railway track diagram showing lines between Manchester Victoria, Bury, Oldham, Rochdale and Todmorden.

Key locations and mileages include:

- BURY 9.51
- Bury Electric Multiple-Unit Depot (BQ)
- Buckley Wells Carriage Sdgs
- Clifton Jn. to Accrington Line
- Hagside LC 8.34 / Dolly Molly LC 8.10
- RADCLIFFE 7.26 — Radcliffe Viaduct
- WHITEFIELD 5.74 — Whitefield Tnl (161 yds) 5.77–6.04
- BESSES-O'-TH'-BARN 5.17
- PRESTWICH 4.42
- HEATON PARK 3.76 — Heaton Park Tunnel (713y)
- BOWKER VALE 3.07
- CRUMPSALL 2.32
- Bury Old Road Tunnel (73 yds) 3.68–3.71
- WOODLANDS ROAD 1.56
- Queens Road Jn 1.38 / Queens Road 1.36
- Smedley Viaduct 1.23
- Queens Rd Tunnel (262 yards)
- Cheetham Hill Jn 0.73
- Collyhurst Tunnel (426 yds)
- Collyhurst Street 1.09
- MANCHESTER VICTORIA 0.00
- Victoria East Jn SB 0.09
- Deal Street Jn 0.43
- 46A: to Ordsall Lane & Salford Crescent
- 45A: to Ashburys & Stalybridge
- West Curve Junction
- Miles Platting 1.50 / Miles Platting Station Jn
- Brewery Sidings SB 1.59
- Newton Heath TMD (NH)
- Diesel Depot
- NEWTON HEATH WORKS — Civil Engineer
- Skew Bridge Sidings
- Thorpes Bridge Jn (TB) 2.23
- Dean Lane 2.54 / DEAN LANE
- Greater Manchester Waste Disposal Agency 2.78
- Quick Mix Concrete Co / Dean Mix Concrete Co
- FAILSWORTH 3.54
- HOLLINWOOD 4.49
- WERNETH Tnl (471 yards) / OLDHAM WERNETH
- Central Tnl (449 yards) / OLDHAM MUMPS 7.40
- Oldham Mumps SB 7.21
- DERKER 8.09
- ROYTON 8.38
- SHAW 10.10 / Shaw Station 10.05
- NEW HEY 11.64
- MILNROW 12.69 / Jubilee LC 11.32
- SMITHY BRIDGE 12.60
- ROCHDALE 10.36 / Rochdale Jn 14.27
- Castleton East Jn 8.53 / Castleton North Jn 8.50 / Castleton South Jn 8.21
- CASTLETON 8.69
- CASTLETON to BOLTON LINE
- MILLS HILL 5.74
- CHADDERTON
- MOSTON 4.00
- Middleton Jn. Sdgs / Vitriol Works SB 4.64
- MIDDLETON JN. to OLDHAM & ROCHDALE LINE
- LITTLEBOROUGH 13.65 — Summit Tunnel (1 mile 1125yds)
- Summit West Tunnel (55 yards)
- Littleboro 14.44 / 15.13
- Greater Manchester PTE boundary
- WALSDEN 17.70
- TODMORDEN 19.13 (W Yorks PTE boundary)
- Hall Royd Jn / 33B: to Burnley
- Millwood Tunnel (225 yds) 19.63–73
- Horsfall Tunnel (274 yds) 20.44–56
- Eastwood 21.34 / 22.62
- LMR ER Regional boundary
- HEYWOOD 1.56 — Powell Duffryn Standard Rly Wagon Co. Ltd.
- CASTLETON (Greater Manchester) Central Materials Depot — Civil Engineer
- MANCHESTER & NORMANTON LINE
- MANCHESTER LOOP
- COLLYHURST CONNECTING LINE NO 2

Key to Viaducts in panel B:
A – Gauxholme No.1
B – Gauxholme No.2
C – Todmorden
D – Lobb Mill
E – Cockden
F – Whitley

(VW) = Manchester Victoria West Jn. SB 0.09

Proposed bridge for East Lancashire Rly

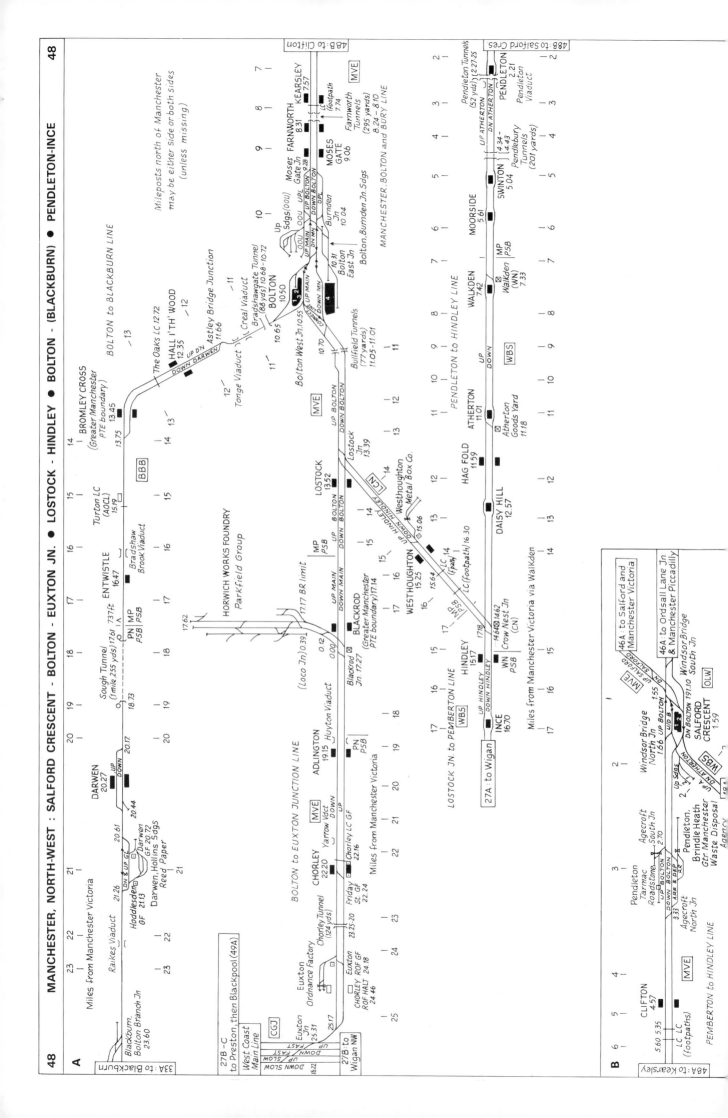

(PRESTON) - BLACKPOOL ● BURN NAZE BRANCH ● BLACKPOOL TRAMWAY ● ORMSKIRK - (PRESTON)

49

FLEETFOOD Ferry
Victoria Street
Ash Street
Copse Road
Broadwater
Rossall
Thornton Gate Pw Yard
Cleveleys
Anchorsholme
Little Bispham
Norbreck
Bispham
Cabin
Gynn Square
Eaves Street
Talbot Square
Tower
Works
RIGBY ROAD
Depot (17 tracks)
South Pier
Sandcastle and Pleasure Beach
Harrowside
STARR GATE

← BLACKPOOL TRANSPORT SERVICES LTD
Electric Tramway

BLACKPOOL NORTH 17.49
Blackpool Carriage Maintenance Depot (BP)
Blackpool North No.1 16.79
Blackpool North No.2 17.30
POULTON to BLACKPOOL LINE
LAYTON 16.32
Carleton Crossing 15.43
Tarn Gate LC 15.59
Thornton LC (TMO) 16.10
Hilly Laid LC (TMO) 16.42
Burn Naze ICI Mond (Hillhouse Works)
Hillhouse No.1 GF 16.63
Hillhouse No.2 GF 17.08
Hillhouse No.3 GF 17.45
Hillhouse No.4 GF 17.61
Burn Naze Hillhouse VCM Sdgs
ICI Chemicals & Polymer Group
Burn Naze ICI Power Station
Oil Sdgs GF
18.77

BLACKPOOL SOUTH 20.01
BLACKPOOL PLEASURE BEACH 19.18
SQUIRES GATE 18.34
ST.ANNES-ON-THE-SEA 16.51
ANSDELL & FAIRHAVEN 14.75
LYTHAM 13.56
SOUTH FYLDE LINE

MOSS SIDE 11.14
Moss Side LC (AOCL) 11.09
KIRKHAM AND WESHAM 7.67
Kirkham South Jn 7.40
Kirkham North Jn 8.29
Kirkham & Wesham Tip CE
KIRKHAM TIP SDG 8.44
Weeton 10.09
Singleton 12.32
POULTON-LE-FYLDE 14.31
Poulton-le-Fylde Jn 14.40
Poulton No.3 SB 14.44

SALWICK 5.17
Salwick (SK) 5.03
Salwick British Nuclear Fuels
PRESTON and FLEETWOOD LINE
Tulketh Viaduct
27C: to Preston

ORMSKIRK 12.15
RUFFORD 17.49
BURSCOUGH JUNCTION 14.61
CROSTON 20.18
Abbey Lane LC 13.43
WALTON JN. to PRESTON LINE
WALTON JN. to PRESTON LINE
42A: to Southport
42A: to Wigan
41A: to Aintree
27C: to Preston

Miles from Liverpool Exchange
Miles from Preston

INDEX TO STATIONS
and Selected Other Places

Station	Code
QUEENS PARK	1
Queens Road	47A
QUORN & WOODHOUSE	17D
RADCLIFFE	6B,47A
Radford Jn	6A/D
RADLETT	2A
Radway Green	13,43A
RAINFORD	41A
RAINHILL	42B
RAMSBOTTOM	30B
Ramsden Dock	31B
RAMSLINE HALT	25C
Ratcliffe	4A
RAVENGLASS	31C,34G
Ravenglass & Eskdale Rly	34G
Ravenhead	42B
Rawdon Colliery	7C
RAWTENSTALL	30B
Rectory Jn	6B
REDDISH NORTH	45A
REDDISH SOUTH	45A
REDDITCH	17E
RHEIDOL FALLS	23E
Rhiw Goch	24J
RHIWFRON	23E
Rhosgoch	37A
RHOSNEIGR	37A
RHYDYRONEN	24E
RHYL	36B
RIBBLEHEAD	34A
RICE LANE	41A
Riddings	5
RIDGMONT	9C
RISHTON	33B
ROBY	42B
ROCHDALE	47A
ROCK FERRY	39A
Rock Savage Works	38A
Rockcliffe Hall	36A
ROCKY VALLEY HALT	24F
ROLLESTON	6B
ROMAN BRIDGE	37D
ROMILEY	45A
Rood End Yard	19
Roodee Jn	35A
ROOSE	31B
ROSE GROVE	33B
ROSE HILL MARPLE	45A
ROTHLEY	17D
Round Oak	20C
ROWLEY REGIS	20C
Royton	47A
RUABON	22C
RUFFORD	49B
RUGBY	11A
RUGELEY	12A
RUNCORN	38A
RUNCORN EAST	26B
RYDER BROW	45A
Ryecroft Jn	19
Rylstone	33C
Saffron Lane	7B
ST. ALBANS	2A
ST. ALBANS ABBEY	8B
St. Andrew's Jn	16,17E
ST. ANNES-ON-THE-SEA	49A
ST. BEES	32A
ST. HELENS CENTRAL	42B
ST. HELENS JUNCTION	42B
St. James	40
St. Luke's Jn	42A
ST. MICHAELS	40
ST. PANCRAS	1
SALE	46A
SALFORD	46A
SALFORD CRESCENT	46A,48B
Salthouse Jn	31B
Saltley	16
Saltney Jn	22D,35A

Station	Code
SALWICK	49A
SANDBACH	43B
SANDHILLS	41A
SANDWELL & DUDLEY	19
Sandycroft	36A
SANKEY	46C
Saughall	35A
SEAFORTH & LITHERLAND	41A
Seaforth Container Terminal	41A
SEASCALE	31C
SELLAFIELD	31C
SELLY OAK	17E
SETTLE	34A
Severn Valley Railway	20C
SHACKERSTONE	34E
Shap	29A
SHAW	47A
Sharnbrook Jn	2D
Sheet Stores Jn	4A/B,6A/C
SHELTON	43A
SHENSTONE	18
SHENTON	34E
SHIRLEY	15A
SHOTTON	36A,37E
Shotton Works	37E
Shotwick	37E
SHREWSBURY	22A,23B
Sherwood Colliery	5
SHIFNAL	21C
Shilton	11A
Siddick Jn	32B
Sileby Jn	4A
SILECROFT	31C
Silkstream Jn	2A
SILVERDALE	31A
Silverdale Colliery	12C
Silverhill Colliery	5
SINFIN CENTRAL	25C
SINFIN NORTH	25C
Singleton	49A
Skelton Jn	46A
Skew Bridge Jn	27C
SKIPTON	33C
SMALL HEATH	15B
Smalmstown	30A
SMETHWICK ROLFE STREET	16
SMETHWICK WEST	16,19
SMITHY BRIDGE	47A
Snowdon Mountain Railway	24F
Soho	16
SOLIHULL	15A
SOUTH HAMPSTEAD	1
SOUTH KENTON	8B
SOUTH ACTON	1
SOUTH WIGSTON	3B
SOUTHPORT	42A
Southwaite	29B
Spekeland Road	40
Spellow	41A
Springs Branch	27A
SPONDON	4B
SQUIRES GATE	49A
STAFFORD	12B
STALYBRIDGE	45A
Standon Bridge	12B
Stanlow & Thornton	35A
Stanton & Staveley	7A
Stapleford & Sandiacre	7A
STAVELEY	28C
Staythorpe	6B
Steamtown	28B
STOKE-ON-TRENT	25B
Stoke Hammond	8A
STOCKPORT	44A
STUBBINS	30B
STYAL	43B
SUMMIT	24F
Sutton Bridge Jn	23B
SWANWICK JN	5
SWINTON	48A
Sydney Bridge Jn	13
SYLFAEN	24D
Syston Junctions	3B

Station	Code
TALYBONT	24B
TAL-Y-CAFN	37C
Talerddig	23D
TALSARNAU	24B
Talyllyn Railway	24E
TAME BRIDGE	19
TAMWORTH	11B, 18
TAN-Y-BWLCH	24J
TANYGRISIAU	24J
Tattenhall	35A
Tebay	29A
TELFORD CENTRAL	22A
THATTO HEATH	42B
Three Spires Jn	14B
THURGARTON	6B
Thornton South Sidings	35A
Thorpes Bridge Jn	47A
TILE HILL	14B
TIMPERLEY	46A
TIPTON	19
TODDINGTON	17A
TODMORDEN	47B
TONFANAU	24A
Toton Yard	7A
TOWN GREEN	41A
TOWN MEADOW	39B
TRAFFORD PARK	46A
TRAETH MAWR	20B
TRAWSFYNYDD	24E
Trent Junctions	4A, 6A
Trent Valley Jns	11A, 12B, 21B
Trentham	12D
TRING	9A
Trowell Jn	7A
Tuebrook Sidings	40
TUNNEL HALT	10C
TUTBURY & HATTON	25C
Tunstead	44A
TY CROES	37A
TYGWYN	24B
Tyn-y-Llwyn Halt	17E
TYSELEY	15B
TYWYN	24A, 24E
TYWYN (PENDRE)	24E
TYWYN (WHARF)	24E
ULVERSTON	31A
UNIVERSITY	17E
UPPER HOLLOWAY	1
UPPERBY	29C
UPHOLLAND	41A
UPTON	39A
URMSTON	46A
UTTOXETER	25C
Vale of Rheidol Railway	23E
VALLEY	37A
VANDYKE ROAD HALT	9D
WALLASEY GROVE ROAD	39A
WALLASEY VILLAGE	39A
Wallercote Sdgs	26A
WALSALL	19
WALKDEN	48A
WALSDEN	47B
WALTON	41A
Walton Old Jn	26B
Walton & Anfield	41A
Watling Streen Jn	1
Warcop	34B
WARRINGTON BANK QUAY	26B
WARRINGTON CENTRAL	46B
WARWICK	14A, 15A
WARWICK ROAD	15B, 46A
Washwood Heath	16
WATERFALL	24F
Watery Road	22D
WATER ORTON	18
WATERLOO	41A

Station	Code
WATFORD HIGH STREET	8
WATFORD JUNCTION	8
Watford Lodge	10
WATFORD NORTH	8
WATFORD STADIUM	8
WATFORD WEST	8
Wavertree	
Weaste	46
Weaver Junction	26
Wednesbury	
Wednesfield Road	1
WEDGWOOD	12
Weeton	49
WELLINGBOROUGH	
WELLINGTON TELFORD WEST	22
WELSHPOOL	23
WELSHPOOL (RAVEN) SQUARE)	24
Welshpool & Llanfair Light Rly	24
WEM	23
WEMBLEY CENTRAL	8
Wembley Intercity	8
WENNINGTON	28
WEST ALLERTON	4
WEST HAMPSTEAD	
WEST HAMPSTEAD THAMESLINK	
WEST KIRBY	39
West Timperley	46
Westbury	23
WESTHOUGHTON	48
Weston Salt Works	38
WHALEY BRIDGE	44
WHATSTANDWELL	
WHISTON	42
Wichnor Jn	
Widnes	38
WIDNES	46
WIDNEY MANOR	15
WIGAN NORTH WESTERN	27
WIGAN WALLGATE	27
Wigston Junctions	3
WIGTON	32
Willesden Brent	8
WILLESDEN JUNCTION	
Willington Power Stn	25
WILMCOTE	15
WILMSLOW	43
WILNECOTE	1
WINCHCOMBE	17
WINDERMERE	28
Winwick Junction	26
WINSFORD	26
Wirksworth Quarry	
Whilton Marina	10
Whitacre Jn	1
WHITCHURCH	23
WHITLOCKS END	15
WHITEFIELD	47
WHITEHAVEN	32
Whitehouse Jn	12
Whitmore	12
Whittington	22
WITTON	1
WOBURN SANDS	9
WOLVERHAMPTON	1
WOLVERTON	9
WOODLANDS ROAD	47
WOOD END	15
WOODLEY	45
WOODSMOOR	44
WOOTTON WAWEN	15
WORKINGTON	32
WRENBURY	23
WREXHAM CENTRAL	22
WREXHAM GENERAL	22
WYLDE GREEN	1
WYTHALL	15
YARDLEY WOOD	15
Yorkshire Dales Railway	34
YORTON	23